Is your child's brain
starving?

Food, *not* drugs, for life and learning

MIND PUBLISHING INC.

Copyright © 2002

Illustrations: Brent Lynch
Photography: Stephen Rank/Ed Park
Design: Stephen Rank

For information contact:
info@naturalmedifaqs.com

ISBN 0-9685168-6-6

Second printing January 2004

Printed in Canada

ABOUT THE AUTHORS

Michael R. Lyon, MD
G. Christine Laurell, Ph.D.

 **Dr. Michael R. Lyon, MD** is a practicing physician and medical researcher with expertise in both allopathic and natural medicine. One of the foremost authorities in the science behind complementary medicine, Dr. Lyon is the Medical and Research Director of the Canadian Center for Functional Medicine. Dr. Lyon has conducted several clinical trials and research projects in the pursuit of better treatments for attention deficit hyperactivity disorder (ADHD).

Dr. Lyon earned degrees in biology and medicine at the University of Calgary, and he completed three years of post-graduate residency training in Oklahoma, Texas, Kansas and British Columbia. He served for four years as an Olympic Team physician and was head of a National Sport Science Committee for Sport Canada. He has written and lectured extensively on subjects such as preventive medicine, sports medicine, nutritional medicine, toxicology and attention deficit hyperactivity disorder.

In addition to publishing in the peer reviewed medical literature, Dr. Lyon is the author of the books "Healing the Hyperactive Brain; through the New Science of Functional Medicine"; and "The Prevention and Treatment of Diabetes with Natural Medicine".

 **Dr. Christine Laurell, Ph.D.** is an environmental health reseacher and educator who has done pioneering work investigating the role of environmental neurotoxins and inadequate nutrition in the development of learning and behavioural problems in school-age children, specifically those deemed to have Attention Deficit Hyperactivity Disorder. She brings over 20 years of teaching and working with children as well as studies in herbology and holistic nutrition to her current practice and research, and is committed to non-drug based approaches to dealing with childhood disorders.

Dr. Laurell is Program Director at the Canadian Center for Functional Medicine where she conducts clinical and school-based programs, as well as research. She holds a Ph.D. in environmental education and a post-graduate diploma from the University of Calgary, as well as a Master of Science from the University of Alberta, and undergraduate degrees in arts and special eduation from Acadia University, Nova Scotia, and the Université de Lausanne, Switzerland. She has taught at the Université de Haute-Normandie, France, Fukushima University, Japan, the University of Alberta, and the University of Calgary, Alberta, Canada.

Why
I Wrote this Book

As the director of a medical research institute, I have explored a variety of potential treatments to improve brain function in children and adults, without the use of drugs like Ritalin.® Although I believe there is promise in certain herbal medicines and in non-drug treatments such as biofeedback, I have seen the most profound improvements in learning and behaviour through an intelligently applied nutritional program.

My goal in writing this book is to make these nutritional changes as simple, easy and enjoyable as possible so anyone can experience a positive transformation. While all of the information in this book is based upon relevant science, technical detail has been kept to a minimum to make this book easy to read and very practical.

Section 1 lays the foundation. Section 2 provides everything practical you need to make this program a success (including recipes, food buying tips and practical guidelines).

I am indebted to Dr. Christine Laurell, Ph.D. for writing the majority of Section 2. Christine brings years of practical experience as a special needs teacher, and her doctoral research in environmental education, which focused on the impact of environmental factors such as nutrition and toxicology on learning and behaviour. Christine also brings to this book a wealth of knowledge from years of teaching those with food allergies how to prepare food that is as enjoyable as it is healthy. Section 2 is a dream come true for anyone who needs to be on a restricted diet. I am sure you will find this section a one-of-a-kind resource for enjoyable allergy-free cooking.

Whether you are reading this book for yourself, for your child or for an elderly loved one, I encourage you to apply these dietary changes to your whole family, as much as possible. Often learning or behavioural problems have a genetic basis and these nutritional principles can benefit every family member. As well, many of the required changes are easier to accomplish if the whole family participates, rather than singling out an individual. Some changes take a bit of getting used to, but with time, these can become healthy habits and a completely enjoyable part of a long and healthy life. Once you have experienced the benefits of smart nutrition, you'll never look back!

Section One

Section Two

transforming
lives through smart nutrition

for more than a decade as a research scientist and practicing medical doctor, I have witnessed the transformational power of good nutrition. It may not surprise you that most of my knowledge of nutrition didn't come from medical school. My interest in nutritional medicine began much earlier, in the 1970s in the "laboratory" of my own body. As a teenager I was dismayed with my own state of health. Overweight and constantly fatigued, I had a troubling heart arrhythmia and numerous allergies. I was a chronic daydreamer with no hope of stellar academic achievement.

Fortunately, I became intrigued with nutrition, exercise and other natural health principles and I began to apply these principles to my own life. Experimenting with some radical dietary changes, I soon realized that my health, my mind and my whole attitude towards life were greatly affected by the foods I ate or did not eat. When I overate, or ate junk foods, fast foods and even some seemingly nutritious foods, I felt awful and my thinking became foggy. It became obvious that if I wanted vigorous health and optimal brain performance I had to change my diet to include natural, whole foods and to eliminate those foods that disagreed with my biochemistry.

Once I made these lifestyle changes, I experienced a remarkable transformation. My health, my personality, and eventually the whole direction of my life shifted. Because of the positive changes in my brain function, learning became easier and my performance at school rocketed skyward. I graduated as the top male student in my high school even though the year before I had been suspended for a whole semester for bad behaviour! That was before I discovered the brain transforming power of nutrition! By maintaining positive health habits I have continued to enjoy vigorous health as well as academic and professional success, through ten long years of university and in my studies and work in nutritional medicine for the last two decades.

I have certainly extended my experience and knowledge beyond the laboratory of my own body. I have seen the impact of positive dietary changes in scores of children and adults, and I am fully convinced that the modern Western diet (as accepted by the typical North American consumer) is completely incompatible with optimal health and good brain function. Although I have witnessed the results of improved nutrition for many health conditions, most of my formal research has focused on the impact of dietary change in children with attention deficit hyperactivity (ADHD) disorder. I have seen children's lives completely turned around through optimal nutrition, again and again.

My own son suffered severely with the symptoms of ADHD. He has now experienced a complete transformation, largely through nutritional changes, and he is now a happy, healthy, well-adjusted boy. And at school? He confidently remains at the top of his class without any behavioural or learning problems.

darlene:
a case study

Reforming A Junk Food Junkie.

darlene reluctantly came to see me, with her mother, when she was fourteen. Previously a quiet, pleasant and successful student, Darlene seemed to be on a downward spiral that had started two years earlier, a spiral that her mother was desperate to reverse before damage to her daughter's future was irreparable. Darlene opposed everything her parents stood for. She was often in trouble at school and her marks dropped so low she would probably have to repeat her current grade. She hated her teachers. She hated school and she felt her mother was a constant nag. She said school was a waste of time and she couldn't wait to get out, get a job and do things her own way. Home from school sick much of the time, she readily admitted that her health was not good.

Darlene also confessed that her diet was atrocious. Her parents were busy managing a family business. For the past two years they had little control over what their daughter chose to eat. Food was just one more thing to argue about, so Darlene's mother gave her money to buy food at school and let her "fend for herself".

Darlene rarely ate breakfast. She flew off to school, grabbed a bag of chips and a can of cola at about 10 am. Lunch often consisted of French fries and gravy and another can of pop. The only real meal she ate was in the evening with her family, but because she usually snacked when she got home from school, her appetite for supper was not that good. Her mother said, "She usually just picks at her food."

Reluctant Reform

Darlene was slightly overweight, had constant headaches, frequently felt weak and dizzy and she couldn't get out of bed before noon on weekends. Her acne had gotten so bad that several layers of makeup didn't help any more.

When I suggested that Darlene needed to eat breakfast and avoid junk food, she protested ferociously. When I pointed out that her many health problems were most likely related to her poor dietary habits, she began to listen. She reluctantly agreed to follow the changes I suggested–but only for one month! If, at the end of our trial month, she didn't feel these changes were worth it, she would go back to doing whatever she pleased. We shook hands on the deal.

Darlene really had trouble eating breakfast, so I prescribed a nutritious Learning Factors Smoothie instead of solid foods. Many people don't eat breakfast because they are in a rush and their stomach is "full of butterflies". Dairy-free breakfast smoothies are well tolerated by people with sensitive stomachs. With the right ingredients, they can also be an excellent source of protein and other brain-critical nutrients. Smoothies any time of day can be easy to digest and a super-nutritious substitute for junkie foods.

For a mid-morning snack Darlene agreed to take some fresh fruit or carrot sticks to school. Though it was tough, she agreed to stay away from pop, French fries and all other junk food at lunch. Instead, she would choose one of the healthy selections from the school cafeteria. If she was hungry after school she would make herself another nutritious smoothie with Learning Factors and some frozen fruit rather than munching on junk food. I gave her and her parents a few recipes for healthy snack foods and suggested they check out their local health food store for healthy snacks (in the case of a junk food emergency!).

The Rewarding Results

After one month Darlene came back to see me with her mom in tow. She marched in beaming. She had gotten As and Bs in all her midterm exams. She had, of her own accord, asked to restart piano lessons (after flatly refusing to play the piano for almost two years). She had joined the school volleyball team and stopped hanging around with the friends her mother did not approve of. Her teacher had sent home a glowing report about Darlene's bright new attitude.

Although initially reluctant to comply with these dietary restrictions, Darlene confessed that she started feeling much better within a few days. The clincher for her came when, after two weeks off junk food, she went with her friends to the mall and had a cheeseburger, fries and a milk shake. That evening she had an awful headache. She got into a big fight with her older brother and she ended up spending the rest of the night crying in her bed. The next morning she could barely get out of bed and she was miserable for the next two days. This was when she told her mother that she realized junk food was like poison and she didn't want to eat it ever again. Her mother was quite amazed at Darlene's discipline. Once she was personally convinced that junk food was no good, she stayed away from it like the plague.

Summary

Darlene's case is typical, not unusual. I have seen similar results many times over. I have also been impressed by how disciplined children and adolescents can be once they acquire sound nutritional knowledge and are aware of the harm they can suffer from unhealthy foods. Once they are fully convinced, I have often found children and adolescents are more steadfast in their resolve to eat properly than their adult counterparts.

the junk food
generation

t he past century has brought about remarkable changes in what Western society considers to be a "normal diet." The vast majority of North Americans have been conditioned to prefer highly processed foods, lacking vital nutrients. Taste is a more important factor in food choices than nutrition. Without knowledgeable, concerned parents, children are particularly likely to adopt a diet governed by taste and convenience. From an early age, children are the prime targets of powerful marketing efforts whose sole purpose is to increase sales of profitable food products. Do you suppose the fact that some of the largest food companies are owned by tobacco "giants" might indicate just how concerned these corporations are with the health effects of their food products?

The average North American consumes too much sugar, too much starch, too much fat and too many synthetic chemicals. They eat too little food containing adequate amounts of vitamins, minerals, trace elements, essential fatty acids, fiber and beneficial plant chemicals. The result? Epidemics of obesity, diabetes, and heart disease to name a few. These are rather obvious to us all, but less obvious are results of unnatural dietary choices on the functioning of the human brain.

The Durable Brain Cell

Unlike most other cells in the body, which are replaced on a regular basis, brain cells must endure and perform for us throughout an entire lifetime. Because the brain is so critical to our survival, the body has mechanisms to keep brain cells alive under nearly any circumstance. When nutritional intake is grossly inadequate, the body still finds a way to feed the brain with the most bare essential nutrients. Even when a person is starving, the brain is kept alive. Other less crucial body cells are sacrificed and molecules, from the breakdown of these cells, are used to keep the brain functioning.

Although the brain is built to survive and perform under adverse nutritional circumstances, optimal brain performance requires optimal nutrition. Brain cells are actually the most sophisticated and demanding cells in the body. They need a wide array of nutrients, available from an intelligently applied nutritional program—like the Smart Nutrition Program outlined further on in this book.

The Sensitive Brain Cell

Brain cells are very sensitive to stress and toxic influences. Many of these toxic influences can enter the body through the diet. Junk food, snack food, fast food and chemically laden processed foods are prime sources of toxic stress on the brain.

Research has shown that the average child gets more than one-third of their daily calories from snack food. Many teenagers consume more than half of their calories as snack foods or fast foods. A recent US Department of Agriculture study noted that French fries and ketchup are the primary "vegetables" in most teenage diets!

The majority of North American children get most of their daily iron and vitamins from packaged breakfast cereals. These are simply sugar coated, artificially flavoured, chemical laced starch, "fortified" with a sprinkling of just a very few of the hundreds of nutrients that were stripped out during processing!

Drive-through style snacks, candy, commercially baked goods, potato chips and other fast foods are veritable icons of our society. Aggressive marketing campaigns are so effective that most of us have come to accept eating at least some junk food as a normal part of life. I have even met parents who consider depriving a child of junk food as tantamount to child abuse.

So What IS Junk Food?

I classify junk food as any food that contains plenty of calories but very few vitamins, minerals, essential fatty acids, fiber or important naturally occurring plant chemicals. Junk foods are high in carbohydrates (sugar or starch) and usually loaded with fats. As well, junk foods are full of chemical preservatives, stabilizers, artificial flavours and colours. Of course junk foods taste best when accompanied by junk beverages, such as sugary soda pop and artificially flavoured and sweetened fruit drinks.

Not all junk foods are commercially prepared, or come in packages. Many of our favourite recipes that "Mom used to make" are clearly junk food. Traditional desserts, homemade deep-fried foods and baked goods made with white flour are just a few of the homemade junk foods many of us crave— they're our "comfort foods".

Feeding your brain, or your child's brain, doesn't necessarily mean abstaining from Grandma's apple pie or Mom's great fish and chips. It does mean cutting way back on such foods. Perhaps the ingredients or cooking methods can be modified to create something that is just as comforting, but much healthier.

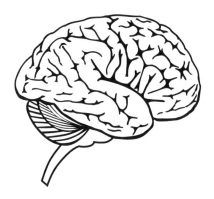

Deep Fried Brain?

You could unwittingly be eating large quantities of chemical food contaminants when you consume junk foods or fast foods. Probably the most harmful of these, especially to the brain, are *altered* fats. Excessive fat of any kind is stressful to the brain, but especially *saturated fat*.

When oil or fat is heated to high temperatures its chemical structure is altered and brain-toxic byproducts are generated.

Foods deep-fried in a commercial or restaurant setting are especially likely to contain toxic byproducts because deep fryer fats are used over and over again.

Did you know that the brain is composed largely of fat? Toxic dietary fats readily assimilate into the brain cells and these toxic molecules can limit, reduce or alter brain function. Anyone who wants a healthy, well functioning brain should steer clear of deep fried food! Since the brains of children are much more sensitive than those of adults, it is even more important for them to avoid deep fried foods.

Another type of brain-toxic altered fat is *hydrogenated vegetable oil*. Hydrogenation is a process where hydrogen is forced into oil molecules at high temperature, turning liquid vegetable oil into thick, heat resistant saturated fat. Although hydrogenation has created vast and profitable markets for vegetable oils, it also creates fats loaded with trans-fatty acids–toxic molecules completely foreign to the human body. Extensive research indicates that trans-fatty acids damage the cardiovascular system, increase cancer risk and generate toxic stress on the brain. *Trans-fatty acids* can be completely avoided by steering clear of deep fried foods and foods that contain *vegetable oil shortening* or *hydrogenated* or *partially hydrogenated vegetable oil*. Such ingredients are clearly listed on food labels when present.

Brain Poisons in our Food

How much poison do you eat in an average week? Recent US government data indicates that the amount of pesticides ingested by the average citizen is far higher than was previously estimated (see www.ewg.org). Liberal use of pesticides in food crops (herbicides, fungicides, and insecticides) is a major threat to brain health. The amount of pesticide residue legally allowed to remain on fresh produce is based upon outdated safety data, considered completely inaccurate by today's standards.

Children are particularly vulnerable to the brain damaging effects of toxic pesticides. Although groups like the American Academy of Pediatrics are working to ban the use of the most brain-toxic pesticides, it will take years, maybe even decades, for these harmful agents to be eliminated from our food supply. Choose organically grown fruits and vegetables whenever possible if you want to stop poisoning yourself and your family.

Certified organic produce is grown without toxic pesticides or chemical fertilizers and it contains higher levels of important micronutrients than chemically fertilized crops. As anyone who chooses organic produce knows, it tastes better too! Going organic can cost a bit more in the short run, but your investment in brain health is going to be worth far more than any money you spend on pesticide-free, nutrient-rich organic produce.

What about GMOs? Additives?

Choosing organic may now be the only way to avoid eating genetically modified organisms (GMOs). Increasingly, agribusiness giants are using genetic engineering to create plants that have some desirable characteristics, but that also contain proteins that may be capable of reacting adversely with the human immune system. Data is sparse but research already suggests that certain genetically modified organisms may contribute to damage or degeneration of the brain.

Soy, tomatoes, corn, potatoes, canola and a host of other agricultural products now primarily consist of genetically modified crops. Unless you want to be part of a very large uncontrolled and potentially very risky experiment being conducted on our world's population, avoid GMOs! Eat organic.

Salt or sugar have been added to foods for centuries. When present in modest amounts, these food additives are relatively benign. However, the quantities commonly added to processed foods contribute significantly to long-term health problems and add to the stresses upon our brain. The average North American consumes hundreds of pounds of salt and sugar every year. Modern food processing technology relies on an incredible collection of synthetic chemicals, most of which have undergone only minimal safety testing. Smart people who care about their brains stay away from synthetic food additives.

Improving the physical functioning of the brain can make an enormous difference in a person's mood, attitude, behaviour and intellectual capabilities. Want a healthy brain? Remove toxic and stressful influences. *Get rid of junk food, pesticides, food additives and GMOs.* Learn to enjoy a diet of wholesome, natural foods, and see the enormously positive impact it can have on your life.

We have put a great deal of work into providing you with lots of creative and flavourful new recipes for main meals and snacks in our recipe section. I rely on health food stores to help me find ways to make a wholesome diet delicious. Health food stores are a fabulous resource for food ingredients, recipe books and delicious alternative snacks. I have great respect for the many knowledgeable health food store owners and workers across North America and Australia. Many of them have struggled with their own dietary transformations. They can help anyone who is seeking to make positive changes to their diet.

cody:
a case study

A Picky Eater Transformed

a t 10 years of age Cody was wired for speed. He never stopped moving, talking or making some kind of sound. Just to be in his presence could raise your blood pressure. Every part of his body was in motion or poised to move. He couldn't stay seated in a chair for more than a few seconds. Even his special education teacher was at the end of her rope with his extreme hyperactive behaviour.

Cody was a classic hyperactive kid. When I met him his future didn't look bright. His hyperactivity and inability to focus were making participation at school impossible. When his pediatrician placed him on Ritalin,® Cody's facial tics became so severe he was diagnosed with Tourette's syndrome. When the doctor switched him to Dexedrine,® he became so grumpy and lethargic that he didn't want to do anything.

His parents came to me to explore drug-free ways to help their child. They were desperate for answers. If they couldn't help him at age 10, what would happen to him as a teenager? If he ended up like so many kids with serious ADHD, his self-esteem would be crushed and he could be at a high risk for drug use and possible criminal behaviour. After spending only a few minutes with Cody, I had to agree that their fears were not unfounded.

Cody's diet was very poor. He rarely ate fruits or vegetables. He liked sugary breakfast cereals, peanut butter sandwiches on white bread, canned spaghetti, macaroni 'dinners' and hotdogs. His parents had grown weary of trying to get him to eat fruits or vegetables because it was always a fight, and they had fallen into the habit of using food treats as a reward for good behaviour. Unfortunately, rewarding children with treats has not been shown to improve eating habits.

Cody was pale, with dark circles under his eyes and dry rough skin; common signs suggestive of food allergies and fatty acid deficiency. Blood tests showed he had a marginal iron deficiency, plus deficiencies in magnesium and zinc. Tests for essential fatty acids and most nutrients, other than minerals, are quite expensive so these tests were not done.

I recommended that his parents begin adding Learning Factors essential fatty acid supplements to his diet, starting with eight capsules per day. He didn't want to take the capsules, but with some gentle and persistent persuasion he was swallowing them without difficulty within three days (as they're quite small). I also recommended that they start making frozen fruit smoothies with Learning Factors Smoothie Mix for him once a day. They tried a few variations until they found the one he liked best, Blueberry Blast, the blueberry smoothie recipe in our recipe book. A gradually increasing dose of Learning Factors Smoothie Mix was added starting with 1/4 of a scoop per serving and increasing to 2 scoops per serving within the first week.

I also gave Cody's parents helpful hints on how to sneak more whole grains, fruits and vegetables into his diet. Bit by bit, with some loving persistence, Cody began to eat a nutritionally exceptional diet instead of his previous, barely survival dietary routine. His parents agreed to cutting out junk foods and replace them with healthy snack foods (like those described later in this book).

The Results

Not months later, but within two weeks there were noticeable changes in this little boy. When he came to see me again he was much calmer, more polite and able to stay seated more easily than on his first visit. His parents were very encouraged. His behaviour at home had improved considerably. His teacher was very happy, as Cody had become much more cooperative in class, less restless and more focused on his work.

Since that time, Cody's parents have learned how to identify and handle Cody's food allergies and intolerances. (There are more details on these subjects in chapters 8 and 9). As Cody's diet was adjusted to eliminate foods that reacted adversely within his body, more and more gains were made. His performance and behaviour at school improved markedly. Today Cody is a happier and better-adjusted boy. His parents no longer feel pushed to control their son with powerful medications.

fueling
the human supercomputer
- brain critical nutrients

Your Brain Is Crying for Good Nutrition

even the most educated health professionals seem to be relatively unaware of the influence and importance of nutrition and brain function. Cattle farmers know how important sophisticated nutrition is to the growth and reproduction of their stock. Bodybuilders understand the critical role nutrition plays in building muscle and cutting fat. Pet owners spend hard-earned money to be sure their beloved companions eat the most beneficial, scientifically engineered diet. Yet even knowledgeable physicians virtually ignore the convincing science that shows how important nutrition is in brain function, behaviour, and overall health.

Still, a few curious scientists and doctors have kept searching for themselves and have applied nutritional principles in their work with patients. The prestigious Center for Science in the Public Interest has released a set of documents entitled "Diet, ADHD and Behaviour: a Quarter-Century Review" (www.cspinet.org). In these documents some of the world's leading experts on ADHD describe how this potentially devastating neuro-developmental disorder can be markedly improved through diet modification. These experts also make it clear that the National Institutes of Health and the National Institute of Mental Health are committed to minimizing, ignoring and ridiculing the ADHD-nutrition connection. They would rather support the use of powerful and profitable drugs to treat this widespread condition.

I know what diet and lifestyle changes did for me. As a physician and medical researcher, I am firmly convinced that most non-optimum brain conditions can be significantly improved through nutritional change. Over the years, I have met hundreds of parents desperate to help their troubled children. In every case these parents come to me earnestly wanting to help their kids without resorting to psychiatric medications like Ritalin.®

Brain Under Siege

Attention deficit hyperactivity disorder (ADHD), autism, obsessive-compulsive disorder, oppositional defiant disorder, and depression have become rampant in today's kids. In fact, a recent Surgeon General's report states that one in ten North American children now suffers from a diagnosable psychiatric condition. What happens when these children grow up? Will their psychological and psychiatric problems be carried over or worsened in their adult life? Without solutions to these conditions, the future of our world is in jeopardy.

Think of this: a very subtle downturn in the overall intelligence of our population would have a profound impact on society. If the average IQ decreased by only five points, the number of individuals officially considered to be mentally challenged/disabled would increase by 50 percent while the number of individuals officially labeled as "intellectually gifted" would decrease by 50 percent (www.igc.org/psr). The whole course of history could change if such a shift were to take place on a global scale.

Certainly there are various factors that have contributed to this dramatic downturn in the health of our children's brains. Genetics alone cannot be blamed. The genetic makeup of our society has remained relatively stable. Environmental factors such as a breakdown in the traditional family, sedentary lifestyles, increased exposure to processed food, pesticides and pollutants as well as dramatic dietary changes are all probable contributors to this downward spiral.

The aging of our population adds greatly to this problem. Experts in the field of neurodegenerative diseases predict that death and disability from conditions such as stroke and Alzheimer's disease will soon exceed the toll from heart disease and cancer. Although age alone is the major risk factor for neuro-degenerative and catastrophic brain disorders, exposure to toxic environmental contaminants and a lack of brain critical nutrients also plays a highly significant role. For instance, it has been shown that the risk of stroke is directly related to a person's lifelong intake of bioflavonoids, (antioxidant plant chemicals) found in fruits and vegetables. Recent research shows that individuals with early Alzheimer's disease can benefit significantly by taking supplements that contain certain vitamins, minerals and pseudonutrients or a-nutrients.

Junk food, contaminants like pesticides and heavy metals, and a decrease in dietary nutrition create a deadly combination against the brain. Parents, are you confident enough to use some old-fashioned discipline to wean your children off junk and help them acquire a taste for nutritious foods? Not long ago parents had little trouble mustering the courage to make their kids swallow a spoonful of foul-tasting cod liver oil every day! Now it seems some parents are afraid to make their kids try a piece of broccoli. As a parent whose children now enjoy broccoli and most other healthy vegetables, I can tell you that persistence and firmness still work.

Nutrition tip 🖊

Recent research has shown that the more frequently a child is exposed to a healthy food (i.e., fruit, vegetables), the more likely he/she will start eating and enjoying healthy food. So continue to put the broccoli and carrots on the dinner table and your kids will eventually eat them.

Feeding the Brain

Optimal brain nutrition begins by eating a truly balanced diet composed primarily of whole, natural foods including plenty of fruits and vegetables. The Canadian Center for Functional Medicine Food Guide provides a good foundation for a healthy diet.

The Canadian Center for Functional Medicine Food Guide

WHOLE GRAIN PRODUCTS ONLY

VEGETABLES

HYDROGENATED OR DEEP FRIED

HEALTHY FATS
(fresh nuts, seeds
olive oil, fish oil, flax
oil. Coconut oil for
sautéing)

DAIRY
(Live culture yogurt,
or kefir or non-dairy
sources of calcium)

FRUITS

LEAN MEAT / FISH / POULTRY / LEGUMES / LENTILS

Choose organically grown foods as often as possible.

Although good nutrition is built on a foundation of a balanced diet, anyone who still believes that we can get all the nutrients we need by simply eating a balanced diet is missing information about the state of our food supply. Most of the fruits, vegetables and grains of today are the byproduct of decades of intense breeding, hybridization and, now, genetic modification. Food crops have been altered to be more uniform in appearance and flavour for the mass market.

Science has done little to improve the nutritional quality of food crops. In fact, the opposite is usually true. Fruits and vegetables today have far lower levels of micronutrients than the same foods had in the past. Artificial fertilizers do not replenish the soil with the range of micronutrients required to ensure high nutritional quality in food crops. As the years go by, artificially fertilized soils become increasingly depleted of trace elements vital to maintaining human health. Also, most produce is transported long distances and harvested before maturity or ripening. The result – food with lower nutritive value.

It seems ironic that in an age when we need peak brain performance more than ever before in history our brains are under attack from every side. Become wise. Avoid brain-toxic influences and provide your brain with optimal nutritional support. This is "food for thought."

Brain Critical Nutrients

Science has identified a number of key nutrients that positively influence brain function. Many people with brain conditions experience significant improvements in cognitive performance, mood and behaviour if they supplement their diet with these brain critical nutrients. Also, anyone who needs to keep their brain performing optimally (and who doesn't?) such as students, executives and the elderly, should optimize their intake of the following key nutritional components:

Essential fatty acids are among the most studied group of brain critical nutrients. The biochemistry behind fatty acid metabolism is extraordinarily complex but we only need to understand a few basic rules to take advantage of these key nutrients.

Essential fatty acids are required by every cell in the human body. They are incorporated into cell membranes and are vital for brain and immune system function. We all require a certain quantity of omega-3 and omega-6 fatty acids from our diets if we want to survive. This is why these fatty acids are called essential. Like vitamins, we need daily minimal allowances of these nutrients to avoid serious deficiency states.

Some nutritionists and dieticians suggest that we can get all the omega-3 and omega-6 fatty acids we need from vegetable oils such as canola or soybean oils. The most commonly available omega-3 fatty acid is known as alpha linolenic acid (ALA) and the commonly available omega-6 fatty acid is known as linoleic acid (LA). Normally, the body must convert ALA and LA into other fatty acids that are then incorporated into the brain and used by the immune system. *Flax oil* is by far the richest source of omega-3 ALA and many people have wisely begun to incorporate this healthy oil into their diets. Unfortunately, in certain cases, the body is inefficient in its conversion of ALA and LA into the fatty acids that it really needs.

The omega-3 fatty acids that the brain and immune system really require are known as docosahexaenoic acid (DHA) and eicosapentaenoic acid (EPA). The only practical sources of DHA and EPA are fish rich in fat such as herring, salmon, tuna and sardines. DHA is especially important in brain function as it is used to build nerve endings in some of the most vital brain regions. Particularly, DHA is required by the areas of the brain that provide us with judgment and the ability to stay focused and complete tasks. *Tuna oil* is the richest commercially available supplement source of DHA. Since tuna meat is often contaminated with mercury and PCBs, it is important to avoid eating too much tuna and, instead, choose tuna oil that has

Nutrition tip

To get more omega-3 fats in your diet, try adding flaxseed oil to salads, vegetables, or other food. For an excellent source of brain beneficial DHA, eat wild caught salmon or sardines at least twice per week.

been verified to be mercury and PCB free. *Salmon oil* (only from wild salmon) and *cod liver* oil are other good sources of DHA. Although difficult to find, cod liver oil free of fishy flavour can be manufactured through a distillation process. This is an excellent source of DHA as well as *vitamins D and A.*

The omega-6 fatty acids needed by the brain and immune system are known as gamma linolenic acid (GLA) and arachidonic acid (AA). AA is relatively common in animal fats and certain vegetable oils. However, GLA is quite uncommon in the diet. The principal source of GLA, for those wishing to increase their intake of this important omega-6 fatty acid, is *evening primrose oil.*

Those who suffer from food allergies, asthma, eczema, heart disease, attention deficit hyperactivity disorder (ADHD) and bipolar affective disorder (manic depression) may be deficient in essential fatty acids, or lacking these nutrients in appropriate ratios.

I recently conducted a research study that examined the essential fatty acid content in the blood of 76 children with attention deficit hyperactivity disorder (ADHD). Low levels of DHA were found in more than 80 percent of the participants, even though most had adequate levels of ALA (the omega-3 fatty acid commonly found in flax and other vegetable oils). This suggested that children with ADHD usually obtain adequate amounts of ALA in their diets but their bodies are unable to convert this ALA efficiently into the brain critical DHA. The area of the brain most affected by ADHD is made up of nerve endings composed of 80 percent DHA. This suggests that children with ADHD should receive supplementary DHA in the form of mercury free tuna oil.

Our study also indicated that 1 in 5 of these same children had inadequate levels of the omega-6 fatty acid GLA, even though they had adequate levels of the other omega-6 fatty acids LA and AA. GLA supplementation would be beneficial in a significant minority of children with ADHD, and since measuring essential fatty acid levels in the blood is very expensive, perhaps the best solution is to give all children a supplement high in both DHA and GLA.

Quality products that contain mercury free tuna oil (DHA) and evening primrose oil (GLA) are now readily available. Learning Factors School Aid essential fatty acid supplements are composed of toxin-free tuna oil combined with evening primrose oil. This product is available in a liquid that can be added by the spoonful to smoothies or taken directly from a spoon. Since this tuna oil is carefully prepared, it has almost no fishy flavour and is quite acceptable to most kids or adults. The same Learning Factors essential fatty acid supplements are also available in softgel capsules that can be easily swallowed.

There has been a good deal of focus and research on the role of essential fatty acids in ADHD and it makes sense to provide optimal levels of these brain critical nutrients in other brain-related conditions. In fact, anyone who wants their brain to function optimally should ensure that they are getting enough essential fatty acids.

PS: More than a Postscript

Although it is not an essential fatty acid, *phosphatidylserine* (PS) is a naturally occurring nutrient that is integral to the structure and function of brain neurons. Vegetable derived PS is now available and it has been shown to significantly improve memory performance in both animal research and double-blind studies in humans. When I need to memorize important information or learn new or complex tasks, I take 200 to 300 milligrams of PS each day for a week or more. I have found that this is one of the most effective ways to improve my memory and mental performance.

Protein made up of *amino acids,* is also an important brain nutrient. Protein acts as a "blood sugar buffer", helping to slow the absorption of sugars into the bloodstream after meals. Meals that are low in protein and high in carbohydrates (starches and sugars) have a tendency to drive blood sugar levels upward initially and can result in rapidly dropping blood sugar levels later on. Studies have indicated that children with behavioural problems commonly have difficulties with blood sugar regulation. Kids can become restless or hyperactive after starchy or sugary meals as their blood sugar rapidly rises, then, as their blood sugar drops, they can become very distracted, moody or aggressive. Eating a good breakfast, high in protein, high in fiber, with moderate carbohydrates (sugar or starch), and moderate amounts of fat, helps keep blood sugar levels from going up and down like a roller coaster. This is one of the main reasons why studies show that eating a good balanced breakfast improves mood, behaviour and academic performance.

Protein is composed of long chains of amino acids. Amino acids provide the building blocks for most neurotransmitters, the molecules brain cells use to exchange information with other cells. The average brain cell sends out branches to 100,000 other brain cells. At the end of each of these branches are nerve endings which rely on the production of neurotransmitters to communicate messages to other brain cells. If a brain cell cannot generate appropriate amounts of neurotransmitters that brain cell cannot function.

Current research clearly demonstrates that deficient or unbalanced neurotransmitter production is at the heart of most brain-related conditions. Depression, bipolar illness, schizophrenia, autism and ADHD are just a few of the many disorders related to abnormal neurotransmitter activity. In attention deficit disorder it has been shown that certain brain regions have low levels of the neurotransmitters dopamine and norepinephrine. Drugs like Ritalin® are used to raise the levels of these neurotransmitters. However, dopamine and norepinephrine are manufactured by the body from the amino acids tyrosine and phenylalanine. These amino acids are abundantly available in certain high protein foods. Starting the day with a high protein breakfast provides these amino acids to meet the brain's neurotransmitter needs for the day.

An Easy Way to Fortify Your Breakfast with Brain-Critical Nutrients

Learning Factors Smoothie Mix is a high protein, highly palatable food powder composed of dozens of brain-critical nutrients. The vegetable-derived protein in Learning Factors Smoothie Mix was chosen for its hypoallergenic properties and because it contains an abundance of tyrosine and phenylalanine, the amino acids used by the body to make the neurotransmitters dopamine and norepinephrine. This protein is excellent brain food; it supports important brain functions such as attentiveness, impulse control and higher judgment. Learning Factors Smoothie Mix is a quick and delicious way to get high quality, brain beneficial protein, along with many other brain-critical nutrients. As well, Learning Factors Smoothie Mix contains vegetable-derived enzymes that aid the digestion of protein. Research has shown that enzymes can improve protein digestion, increasing the availability of important amino acids by as much as 50 percent.

At the time of this writing, Learning Factors Smoothie Mix has been developed in two versions, a natural unflavoured mix and a naturally berry flavoured, naturally sweetened version. The naturally flavoured and sweetened version is popular with kids, and adults may find it acceptable just mixed in a shaker with water for a quick snack or meal replacement. For best taste however, both versions can be used as the base for a delicious fruit smoothie providing the nutritional benefits of the fruit as well. The natural unflavoured version of Learning Factors Smoothie Mix is slightly superior nutritionally, with higher levels of protein and no added sweeteners. It should be made using an appropriate recipe from our recipe section.

Whichever Learning Factors Smoothie Mix you use, this product is the result of painstaking research and highly technological manufacturing processes designed to ensure the potency of each ingredient. Learning Factors Smoothie Mix provides optimal quantities of the following nutrients:

Brain-Critical Minerals and Trace Elements

■ *Iron* is used by the body for more than building blood cells. Iron is located at the heart of powerful enzymes known as cytochromes that are housed within cellular energy "generating stations" known as mitochondria. Every cell contains mitochondria, and brain cells, which require enormous amounts of energy, are packed with these tiny powerhouses. The areas of the brain responsible for attentiveness, impulse control and higher judgment are also the most complex and energy-demanding brain regions. Not surprisingly, they have the highest density of cytochromes. Research has shown that children with marginal iron deficiencies tend to have problems with attentiveness, behaviour and intelligence even if the iron deficiency is not sufficient to cause anemia. It has also been demonstrated that iron supplementation improves behaviour and cognitive performance in such cases. Learning Factors Smoothie Mix is enriched with a highly absorbable form of iron.

■ *Calcium*, apart from its role in bone structure, is vital in stimulating the activity of brain neurons. As well, calcium is involved in hundreds of other cellular processes. It is very important for everyone to obtain adequate amounts of calcium in a highly absorbable form. Unfortunately, many children and adults with brain related difficulties are also intolerant to calcium rich dairy products. They often dislike calcium rich vegetables such as broccoli, kale and Brussels sprouts. To make matters worse, recent data from the FDA suggests that many commercially available calcium supplements are contaminated with lead! Natural Factors Nutritional Products Ltd. (a North American supplement manufacturer; makers of Learning Factors) follows stringent quality control measures to ensure that lead or other heavy metals are not present in any of their products. Learning Factors Smoothie Mix is an excellent dairy-free source of calcium and is rigorously tested to ensure it is lead-free.

■ *Magnesium* is a mineral required in more than 500 different biochemical processes within the body. This important nutrient has a calming influence over nerve and muscle cells. When magnesium levels are low, nerve cells become irritable and muscle cells become increasingly tense. Research has demonstrated that magnesium supplementation helps diminish hyperactive behaviours in children with ADHD. In my practice I find that marginal magnesium deficiency is very common in hyperactive kids. Poor dietary intake, combined with excessive loss of magnesium from the kidneys, is probably responsible for this phenomenon. High levels of stress hormones (cortisol and adrenaline) lead to excessive magnesium losses from the body. Children or adults with behavioural, mood or intellectual problems, as well as people under high levels of stress, probably all experience excessive stress hormone production. Unfortunately, once magnesium levels are less than ideal, the muscle tension and brain irritability that result contribute even further to production of stress hormones. Magnesium supplementation is a wise measure to support brain function in anyone under stress or dealing with brain related problems. Learning Factors Smoothie Mix is an excellent source of highly absorbable magnesium.

■ *Zinc* is another mineral with hundreds of functions in human biochemistry. It is especially important in immune and gastrointestinal system function. Studies indicate that children with ADHD often have low levels of zinc and respond positively to zinc supplementation. In clinical practice I frequently detect marginal zinc deficiency in children with learning or behavioural problems.

■ *Trace elements* also affect brain function. *Chromium* is an element that is frequently deficient in the North American diet. This nutrient is very important in maintaining control of blood sugar levels. *Selenium* is a trace element needed for antioxidant protection, detoxification from environmental contaminants and for proper thyroid function, all of which directly affect brain health. Learning Factors Smoothie Mix was engineered to contain optimal quantities of zinc, chromium, selenium and other important minerals and trace elements.

■ *B Vitamins*, especially thiamin (B1), pyridoxine (B6), folic acid and vitamin B12, are all brain critical nutrients. These vitamins are important for energy generation and since the brain consumes 25 percent of the body's energy, they are vital to brain function. Vitamins B6 and B12 also have direct roles in neuronal biochemistry. Learning Factors Smoothie Mix is enriched with very high levels of all the important B vitamins.

■ *Antioxidants* provide protection against a form of biochemical wear and tear known as oxidation. Oxygen is absorbed continuously into the body. It reacts with food molecules and releases energy to drive the machinery of life. However, an apple turns brown when it is cut open and exposed to oxygen, molecules within the body are susceptible to damage by "inappropriate" reactions with oxygen. Researchers around the world now agree that excessive oxidation is the primary factor in aging and ultimately death. Poor nutrition, exposure to toxins, over-activation of the immune system and excessive stress, all dramatically increase oxidative stress within the body. Mounting research suggests that non-optimum brain conditions are at least partly related to excessive oxidation. Supporting and protecting the body with antioxidants helps diminish oxidative stress upon the brain and may result in significant improvements in brain function. *Vitamin C, vitamin E, beta-carotene, and selenium* are all important antioxidants. *Grape seed extract* contains numerous bioflavonoids, (natural plant chemicals that are potent antioxidants) which readily penetrate the brain. *Decaffeinated green tea extract* is another excellent, brain beneficial antioxidant. Learning Factors Smoothie Mix contains significant amounts of these brain beneficial antioxidants.

■ *Phytochemicals* are the multitude of beneficial plant-derived chemicals that are abundant in nature, and in a diet rich in whole grains, fruits and vegetables. Until quite recently, nutritional research ignored phytochemicals, focusing only upon vitamins and minerals. Unlike vitamins and minerals, most phytochemicals are not essential to life. Severe deficiency diseases will not result when these nutrients are absent. However, phytochemicals are indispensable for optimizing human performance and diminishing the risk of disease. Phytochemicals also contribute significantly to optimal brain function.

Cruciferous vegetables (broccoli, cabbage, etc.), grapes, berries, onions, garlic, green tea, and traditional herbs and spices are just a few of the phytochemical rich natural foods that should be plentiful in one's diet. Our culture's fondness for processed, overcooked and chemically adulterated food means that many people's diets are sorely lacking in life-giving phytochemicals. Our recipe section contains many delicious ways to increase the phytochemical content of your diet. Nutritious smoothies are one of the easiest and most acceptable ways to increase the intake of brain-friendly phytochemicals. Learning Factors Smoothie Mix is enriched with beneficial phytochemicals including grape seed extract, green tea extract (described under antioxidants above), milk thistle extract and lemon oil. When used as directed, in combination with fresh or frozen fruit, Learning Factors is a quick and easy way to add phytochemicals to your diet.

Potent green food extracts, such as Natural Factors Enriching Greens, are another source of valuable phytochemicals. I add a spoonful of Enriching Greens powder to fruit smoothies for added health support. Enriching Greens can also be taken in capsules or mixed with juice.

■ *Detoxification nutrients* are dietary components necessary for proper processing and elimination of undesirable waste materials and environmental pollutants from the body. Environmental as well as internally generated neurotoxins may represent the greatest overall threat to human brain function. Therefore, strategies to improve the body's ability to eliminate neurotoxins are key for long-term brain health. Learning Factors Smoothie Mix provides sophisticated biochemical support for detoxification. This product contains ingredients such as glycine, n-acetylcysteine, L-glutamine, and inorganic sulfate. These nutrients are used by liver cells to process waste materials and 'package' them for efficient excretion. Milk thistle extract, a well-researched botanical medicine, provides antioxidant bioflavonoids that concentrate within the liver. These bioflavonoids stimulate detoxification within the liver while protecting the liver cells from toxic oxidative stress and stimulating the flow of waste laden bile from the liver into the intestine.

Learning Factors Smoothie Mix also provides dietary fiber (soluble and insoluble). Besides the benefits of fiber for digestion, dietary fiber clings to toxins expelled by the liver through the bile and hastens their removal from the body through the feces. Without adequate dietary fiber, toxins released from the liver into the intestine would be reabsorbed back into the bloodstream in large quantities.

Recap:

Brain Critical Nutrition Made Simple

Learning Factors School Aid -
Essential Fatty Acid Supplements*

Age	First 3 months	Long Term Maintenance
2-6	6 capsules per day	4 capsules per day
7-12	8 capsules per day	6 capsules per day
12+	10 capsules per day	8 capsules per day

Learning Factors Smoothie Mix

Age	First 3 months	Long Term Maintenance
2-6	1/2-1 scoop per day	1/2-1 scoop per day
7-12	1-2 scoops per day	1-2 scoops per day
12+	2-4 scoops per day	2-4 scoops per day

1 teaspoon of the Learning Factors School Aid essential fatty acid liquid supplement is equivalent to 5g of oil or 4 capsules of the Learning Factors School Aid in softgel capsules.

What's the foundation for intelligent nutrition? Avoid junk food. Rely on wholesome natural foods, preferrably certified organic. Supplement with essential fatty acids and other brain critical nutrients. While I was working on creating Learning Factors Smoothie Mix, my goal was to make smart nutrition as easy as possible for children and adults. By incorporating Learning Factors Smoothies into one's diet, and Learning Factors essential fatty acid supplements, children and adults can easily achieve improved brain function. If the dozens of brain critical nutrients in Learning Factors were purchased separately, the cost and complexity of such a program would be overwhelming for most people. Learning Factors makes optimal brain nutrition achievable for almost everyone.

james:
a case study

Miracles can Happen at Any Age

at 28 years of age, James had never been able to hold down a job. Adopted by well-to-do parents as an infant, James had health problems from a very early age. He was on antibiotics for ear infections almost continuously until he was 10. He also had a speech impediment, abdominal pain, headaches and asthma. James was hyperactive with a very poor attention span so he was labeled "learning disabled." Put in a special class and given Ritalin® for 8 years, it's no surprise that James quit school in grade 10 after repeating 3 grades in spite of his parents' efforts to help him. Specialists were unable to give his parents any real solutions to his problems. James didn't seem able to focus on any kind of training. At 18 he left home and began wandering the streets. Homeless much of the time, he survived on welfare and occasionally turned up on his parent's doorstep, begging for help. Unfortunately, James was also a compulsive gambler, so any money he was given would be gone very quickly and he'd end up back on the street.

James' father told me he would do anything to help his son, in fact he had already done a great deal. My recommendations were quite simple. James needed to be assessed for nutritional deficiencies, leaky gut syndrome, food allergies and intestinal parasites. Testing revealed that he indeed had a leaky gut, serious nutritional deficiencies and problems with intestinal parasites. He was placed in a private group home with a dedicated support worker to help him make the necessary lifestyle changes.

James was treated using the Smart Nutrition Program outlined in this book. Within 3 months miracles began to occur. For the first time in his life, James began to shower every day without being forced. He lost 20 pounds and began to sleep through the night, another first. He began to speak more clearly and he read books for the first time. By the fourth month James was a new person. He lost interest in gambling and got a job 20 hours per week stocking shelves in a retail store. After one month on the job he moved to full time. The care worker who was assigned to help James was astounded. He had never seen anything even remotely resembling the transformation he observed in those 4 months. And James' parents? They were, and are, very grateful to see their son happy, healthy and embarking on a new and productive life. James is a perfect example of the tremendous power of the gut –immune–brain connection.

get on board:
the gut - immune - brain - connection

So much of what we learn about the body in medical school — or even as parents — is based on its careful division into separate organs and body systems. Modern medicine tends to progress along these lines with many "fields of specialization." However, in spite of remarkable advances in real research, it is increasingly clear that the body is a highly integrated unit in which all organs and systems work together. On the other hand, when one body system is disordered, that disorder can ripple through and affect every body system.

For example, the brain and immune system are intimately connected by a high-tech communication network. Brain cells communicate to one another by releasing packets of molecules known as neurotransmitters, in an orderly system that is like a molecular language. Amazingly, cells of the immune system possess receptors that can understand the language of the neurotransmitters. Immune cells can also generate and release these same neurotransmitters and many of their own specialized chemical messengers. So, the brain can "hear" and understand messages from the immune system, and the immune system "hears" what the brain has to say.

Did you ever get a cold or flu after a period of intensive emotional stress? Often emotional stress experienced by the brain results in an exhaustion of the immune system, leaving us more susceptible to infection. Conversely, the chemical messengers released by the immune system have a significant influence on brain function. How do you feel when you catch the flu? It's not the flu virus that makes you irritable, foggy in the brain and fatigued. It is actually the chemical messengers from the immune system that create unpleasant flu symptoms as they try to counteract the invaders.

And the Gut?

Similarly, the gastrointestinal tract has enormous influence over both the immune system and the brain. Did you know that more than half the cells in the immune system are located in and around the gastrointestinal tract? When the gut is under stress, the immune system is immediately affected. The two systems, immune and digestive, send out chemical messengers of alarm that enter the bloodstream and affect the brain.

Leaky Gut Syndrome

Under normal circumstances, the lining of the small intestine is nearly leak proof and only fully digested food molecules are permitted to pass through this lining into the bloodstream and lymph vessels. It is very fortunate that the intestine is leak proof. The world within the stomach and intestines is full of hostile elements: powerful acid, digestive enzymes, undigested food material and trillions of microorganisms. To inject even a small amount of the contents of the digestive tract into the bloodstream would be very unhealthy indeed. The lining of the intestine shields us and allows only the absorption of molecules that are needed by the body.

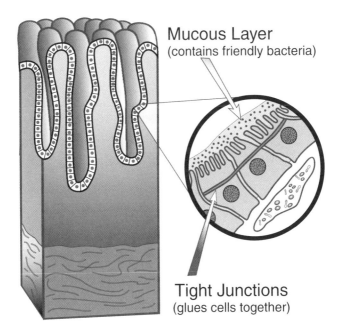

Mucous Layer
(contains friendly bacteria)

Tight Junctions
(glues cells together)

However, this leak proof lining is only one cell layer thick and can be easily damaged. The cells of this lining live only three days. They have extremely high metabolic activity and intense nutritional demands. All the cells lining the intestine are joined by sticky belts around their middles known as tight junctions. If stresses on these delicate cells are too severe, the tight junctions begin to detach, and gaps form between the cells. Every gap becomes a microscopic passageway for larger molecules that go, undigested, into the bloodstream and lymph vessels of the intestine. If enough of these gaps occur the stage is set for "increased intestinal permeability" or "leaky gut".

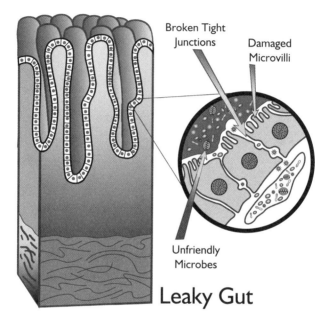

Broken Tight Junctions

Damaged Microvilli

Unfriendly Microbes

Leaky Gut

Leaky gut syndrome allows large quantities of molecular debris – undigested and partially digested protein, carbohydrate and fat as well as fragments from microorganisms – to pollute the blood and lymph of the intestinal tract. Some of this debris is transported to lymph nodes or to the liver, which then has to digest, process and remove it. Some of this material ends up circulating in the body. All of this puts a great strain on the immune system, the liver and virtually every other organ and system of the body.

Leaky gut syndrome often follows critical illnesses, trauma, burns or major surgery. It can also accompany chronic illnesses such as alcoholism, Crohn's disease, food allergies, eczema and arthritis. In all of these cases, the "leakier" the gut, the worse the prognosis for the patient. Leaky gut syndrome has also been found in cases of autism. As well, research that I have conducted recently shows that most children with attention deficit hyperactivity disorder suffer from a leaky gut.

Many health practitioners agree, leaky gut syndrome can cause a wide range of problems, including: fatigue, irritability, hyperactivity (in some children), lethargy, mood swings, muscle or joint pain, poor concentration, memory difficulties, sleep disturbances, food hypersensitivities and environmental intolerances.

What Causes a Leaky Gut?

Consider this list of the things that can cause or contribute to a leaky gut, many of which are highly modifiable: nutritional deficiencies, severe emotional stress or trauma, drug use (especially antibiotics and anti-inflammatory drugs), alcohol abuse, gastrointestinal parasites, intestinal bacterial infections or overgrowth, ingestion of junk foods (especially deep fried foods or those made with hydrogenated vegetable oils), excessive consumption of starchy or sugary foods, and food allergies.

One major junk food binge or a single course of antibiotics may create a leaky gut condition within hours. If the diet then lacks the proper nutritional support to repair the injured gut lining, or if the irritation continues, leaky gut syndrome can become a persistent problem.

Testing for Leaky Gut Syndrome

It is possible to test for leaky gut syndrome, usually by a test known as the lactulose-mannitol intestinal permeability test. Many nutritionally oriented medical doctors or natural healthcare providers use this test. Although it is relatively inexpensive, this testing is generally used as a research tool and is not currently covered by most insurance providers.

Food is Information

Everyone knows that food is used by the body to make energy, and to build and rebuild organs. However, it might come as a surprise that food is also an important source of information. It communicates life-giving messages to our cells. For example, dietary fiber, fermented into small molecules (short chain fatty acids) by bacteria in the colon travels to the liver and "tells" the liver to increase its detoxification activities, helping the body dispose of undesirable pollutants. Likewise, molecules in whole grains and legumes "speak" to the liver and instruct it to decrease its production of cholesterol. Magnesium "communicates" to the blood vessels telling them to relax, lowering blood pressure. Bioflavonoids, plant chemicals found in fruits and vegetables, "instruct" brain cells to increase their production of neurotransmitters, improving brain function. Omega-3 fatty acids "converse" with our cells and encourage them to cool it with the inflammation!

There are thousands of examples of how natural, health-giving foods "speak" this amazing molecular language understood by our bodies. In a very real way, natural food is full of intelligence. In contrast, fast foods, junk foods and over-processed foods can be considered unintelligent, and illiterate, because they lack important phytochemicals, fiber, vitamins and minerals. They lack the messages the body depends upon.

Junk food is not the only thing that disrupts the exchange of biochemical information. Leaky gut syndrome may also cause a flood of wrong messages to be communicated from the digestive system to the body. For example, when casein protein from milk, or gluten protein from wheat, are partially digested, they can form fragments known as peptides that have powerful morphine-like properties if injected into the blood. These peptides, also known as exorphins, are similar to peptides made by the body called endorphins, which also have powerful morphine-like properties. In infants, who generally have a leaky gut, exorphins enter the bloodstream after nursing and have a calming effect, but in children and adults with leaky gut, exorphins circulate after wheat or dairy foods are eaten. They can accumulate and cause undesirable drug-like or toxic effects upon the brain. As well, since foods containing dairy or wheat are such a common part of the modern western diet, leaky gut syndrome may be responsible for addictions to wheat or dairy products as well as withdrawal symptoms when these exorphin-containing foods are eliminated.

Virtually all foods have the potential to cause molecular confusion in the body. Science is just starting to recognize and measure the range of drug-like, toxic or immunological effects exerted by poorly digested food in those with leaky gut syndrome. We have a lot more to learn. What is clear, is that optimal digestion, good nutrient absorption and a leak proof gut are essential for good health.

The Amazing World Within: The Microbial Universe

Our bodies have important, symbiotic (mutually beneficial) relationships with specific kinds of microbes. In the gastrointestinal tract of an average person, approximately 400 species of bacteria and several species of yeast can be commonly found. Many of these organisms play important roles in our digestive and immune system functions. Other species may be neither beneficial nor harmful, while some can be downright nasty!

Our bodies contain a lot of cells, but even more bacteria. If you could take a census of the cells in your body, bacteria would outnumber human cells by ten times – 1,000,000,000,000,000 bacterial cells vs. 100,000,000,000,000 human cells. In fact there are more bacteria in our bodies than there are stars in the known universe! We coexist, happily or not, with our bacterial inhabitants and can benefit tremendously from their presence. When we're healthy the immune system selectively "farms" beneficial bacteria while it tries to make life difficult for unfriendly bacteria, yeasts and parasites.

The Amazing War Within: Good Guys/Bad Guys

The body works hard to suppress the growth of *harmful gut microbes*. Stomach acid, mucous, bile, digestive enzymes and large quantities of antibodies all help suppress unfriendly bacteria, yeasts and parasites. On the other hand, the human digestive and immune systems support the growth of friendly bacterial species known as probiotics. If present in high enough numbers, these healthy probiotics help to suppress the growth of less desirable microbes.

Many illnesses can be blamed on *harmful microbes*. Patients who are critically ill often lack friendly (probiotic) gut bacteria and have instead, an overgrowth of harmful (pathogenic) gut bacteria. Less severe disease states have also been shown to occur due to the immune system's failure to suppress harmful microbes. Stomach ulcers were previously thought to be caused by stress. However, it is now clear that most ulcers are caused by the overgrowth of a harmful (pathogenic) gut bacteria known as Helicobacter pylori. Other research has shown that autism, arthritis, heart disease, chronic fatigue syndrome, fibromyalgia and irritable bowel syndrome may all have some relationship to the type and quantity of microorganisms inhabiting the gastrointestinal tract and found elsewhere throughout the body.

Intestinal microbes can dramatically modify the functioning immune system. For example, intestinal parasites have been shown to "turn on" or "tune up" the immune system's allergy response. In fact, people can develop food allergies for the first time after they've been infested with intestinal parasites. There are cases on record of whole families who mysteriously developed food allergies and were later found to be infected with intestinal parasites.

Gut microbes also have the potential to influence brain function. Microbes compete for territory by producing toxic chemicals. Some of these chemicals, such as the lactic acid produced by friendly (probiotic) bacteria, are harmless or even beneficial to humans. Other, less desirable gut inhabitants have the potential to produce molecules toxic to the human gut wall, liver, immune system, muscles or brain. Most unfriendly microbes are present in numbers too small to create any significant toxic stress. However, if their numbers increase, and especially if the gut is leaky, these pathogens may cause real problems with brain function and overall health.

The Probiotic-ADHD Connection

Research I conducted on 75 children with ADHD showed that the majority of these kids had little or no friendly (probiotic) gut bacteria, but all had high amounts of potentially harmful (pathogenic) bacteria within their bodies. About one third of these kids were also found to have colonies of potentially pathogenic yeast, and nearly half had one or more intestinal parasite. Some kids had as many as five different species of intestinal parasites! The same research showed that these disturbances in the ecology of gastrointestinal tract are usually accompanied by leaky gut syndrome, allowing microbial invaders to do even more harm.

My research also identified specific immune system weaknesses in more than 80 percent of children with behavioural or cognitive problems. Leaky gut syndrome, lack of probiotic gut bacteria and nutritional inadequacies almost certainly play a significant role in this reduced immunity. I am convinced that every person who suffers with brain related difficulties is likely to be suffering from some combination of immune system deficits, loss of probiotic flora and predominance of pathogenic gut organisms. These ARE *reversible* conditions.

The Importance of Probiotics

Humans thrive on intimate relationships. This is true on a personal level in our family and social networks but it is also true of our cells on the microscopic level. Probiotic bacteria have an intimate and mutually beneficial relationship with our intestinal and immune cells. These "friendly flora" help us to digest food, to generate important nutrients; they modulate the immune system, they diminish allergic reactivity, and they prevent the reproduction and colonization of undesirable microbes. As well, probiotics neutralize toxins in the gut and stimulate gut wall healing in those with a leaky gut. With all of the benefits that they provide, it is actually amazing that we can survive at all without rich populations of probiotic gut bacteria.

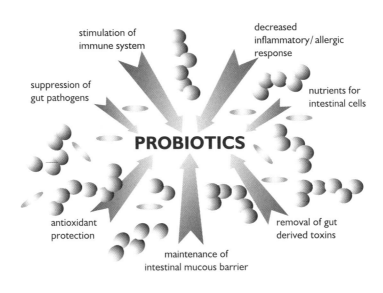

Bifidobacteria

A healthy breast-fed infant has perfect gut flora. Their colon is populated predominantly by *Bifidobacteria*. This probiotic organism can program the immune system to fight infection efficiently while lowering allergic responsiveness. There are good reasons to believe that breastfeeding helps prevent food allergies from developing partly because it promotes growth of colonic *Bifidobacteria*. Research now suggests that children with adequate quantities of *Bifidobacteria* are less likely to develop allergic diseases such as asthma. These probiotics may even help prevent childhood cancers such as leukemia. Although Bifidobacteria remains the star of the probiotic world, an assortment of other lactic acid producing probiotics take up residence within the human gut as we age and they provide additional benefits to their human host.

Unfortunately, antibiotics, bottle feeding, junk food/fast food, lack of dietary fiber and nutritional insufficiencies can all kill off our probiotic bacteria and increase the populations of undesirable microorganisms. Abdominal pain, excessive gas, diarrhea, constipation, food allergies or intolerances, asthma, eczema, fatigue, irritability, and cognitive difficulties are just a few of the many indications of a probiotic/pathogenic imbalance.

Using Therapeutic Probiotics

The benefits of supplementing with probiotic bacteria are increasingly recognized by the scientific community. In fact, research into the benefits of probiotics has been expanding rapidly and one of the important facts that has been revealed is that only very specific strains of bacteria are highly effective probiotics. Traditionally yogurt, or yogurt bacteria, have been best known including various strains of *Lactobacillus acidophilus, Lactobacillus bulgaricus* or *Bifidobacteria.* However, most of these strains, when studied, do not survive in the human gastrointestinal tract when taken as a supplement and their benefits can be mild and transient. Certainly there are benefits to eating live culture fermented dairy products but their benefits are minimal compared to newly discovered "super-strain" probiotics.

Impressive new research from medical schools around the world has begun to show the superiority of a few specific strains of probiotic bacteria. Advanced genetic techniques are used to identify the exact desirable strain amongst the thousands of different strains in a given bacterial species. Although there are tens of thousands of different strains of *Lactobacillus acidophilus,* for example, only a handful are ideal for oral supplementation. These are the strains that can survive passage through the human gastrointestinal tract and have a wide range of health promoting qualities. *Lactobacillus rhamnosus* is a species that contains some of the most impressive strains of scientifically validated probiotics. When taken as a dietary supplement, *Lactobacillus rhamnosus* can markedly diminish symptoms in those with food allergies. For those with food allergies this is a truly revolutionary discovery because, up until now, there has been little offered to help the food allergy sufferer. A highly effective strain of *Lactobacillus rhamnosus* is the key bacteria found in most of the probiotic products made by Natural Factors Nutritional Products Limited, a leading North American supplement manufacturer.

An exciting new breakthrough in probiotic research is the discovery of two strains of bacteria from the species known as *Propionibacterium freudenreichii* (together they are known commercially as Propio-Fidus™). Propio-Fidus™ stimulates the growth of various strains of *Bifidobacteria* for many important benefits; primarily stimulating the gastrointestinal immune system. However, *Bifidobacteria* are very fragile and, if taken orally, only a tiny percentage survive to populate the intestinal tract. Propio-Fidus™ taken orally can dramatically stimulate the growth of the star probiotic, Bifidobacteria. This "bifidogenic" property makes Propio-Fidus™ unique in the probiotic world and it is now classified as the world's first "symbiotic" bacterial supplement. Since *Bifidobacteria* is probably the most important inhabitant of the human gut, finding a way to reliably and dramatically increase its population is truly an important breakthrough.

Propio-Fidus™ is also unique in that it generates a byproduct known as propionic acid. Unlike the lactic acid produced by most probiotic bacteria, propionic acid is a very potent, but nontoxic, yeast-suppressing substance. This yeast killing property may just set Propio-Fidus™ apart as the most important probiotic available in the practice of natural medicine.

A few years ago I conducted research that showed about one third of children with attention deficit disorder had an overgrowth of the yeast Candida albicans in their intestinal tracts. This isn't surprising since many kids with ADHD have weakened immune systems and, as a result, have been given several courses of antibiotics. Many health practitioners believe that overgrowth of the common Candida yeast can cause or worsen common health problems such as environmental sensitivities, fatigue, irritability, mood swings, hyperactivity and inattentiveness. Although most in the medical profession deny the significance of the yeast connection in human health problems, scientific literature contains evidence of the toxic nature of this common fungus.

Propio-Fidus,™ with its anti-yeast, pro-Bifidobacteria properties, is one of the most promising natural therapeutic agents we have to help rid the gut of undesirable microbes and to reestablish healthy gut flora. Propio-Fidus™ is found in a product called InnerSync,™ made by Natural Factors Nutritional Products Limited.

Help the Brain: the **ANT PIE** Program!

Hopefully, you now understand that brain health and gut health are vitally linked. Whether you are a student who wants top marks, a senior concerned about preserving your youthful brain function or a parent earnestly wanting to help your learning or behaviourally challenged child, digestive system health is of utmost importance. Improve gut fitness and see brain-related improvements!

An effective gastrointestinal rehabilitation program I developed to recommend to patients and teach to healthcare professionals, is called the ANT PIE Program. This may sound silly but as an acronym for the program's component parts, it makes remembering the steps in the program a lot easier.

ABSTAIN:

Start by abstaining from the most obvious gut offenders. *Junk food, fast food, deep-fried, overcooked, over-processed, and most canned foods, should be the first to go. Avoid products containing hydrogenated vegetable oils.* They are harmful to the delicate lining of the intestine. Reduce amounts of dietary fat, sugar or starches. Replace coffee, sugary soft drinks and fruit juices with water, green tea or herbal tea. If you frequently indulge in these health-sapping foods, you may have some tough habits to break but once you experience the benefits of eating a healthy, whole foods based diet, it will be hard to go back. Also cool it on bad habits such as skipping meals, eating too much before bed, overeating, or eating when not hungry. As far as possible avoid substances like anti-inflammatory drugs, antibiotics, and more than small amounts of alcohol.

NOURISH:

Intestinal cells have high nutritional demands. They need a foundation of whole foods like whole grains, vegetables and fruits. Good quality protein, vitamins, minerals, trace elements, essential fatty acids, fiber and a variety of phytochemicals are all highly important when trying to heal a leaky gut. *L-glutamine* is a key intestinal nutrient that needs to be included in any gut rehabilitation program. *Zinc, antioxidants (such as vitamin C, vitamin E, beta-carotene, grape seed extract, milk thistle extract and green tea extract), water soluble fiber (such as guar gum), lecithin and omega-3 fatty acids* from fish oil and *flax oil* are all key nutrients that can help a leaky gut recover. As well, because leaky gut is associated with decreased nutrient absorption, supplementation with calcium, magnesium, selenium, chromium and other important trace elements is very important. Finally, dietary enzymes are often recommended by nutritional practitioners to improve digestive processes in those with leaky gut.

TOXINS (get rid of them!):

The kidneys, small intestine, colon and liver carry the enormous burden of keeping the body free of thousands of different toxins. Some of these are chemicals generated by normal metabolism; other toxins are produced by microbes within the gut; while still others are absorbed through air, water or food. Exercise promotes good digestion and helps effective detoxification. Certain nutrients can help the liver and gut efficiently dispose of toxins and can relieve toxic stress on the gut, immune system and brain. The amino acids *glycine, taurine, N-acetyl cysteine,* and *L-glutamine* are *key liver detoxification nutrients,* along with *inorganic sulfate.* The plant antioxidants found in extracts from green tea, milk thistle and grape seed protect the gut and liver, while stimulating detoxification activities. Calcium, magnesium, zinc, selenium, folic acid, thiamine and vitamin B6 are also active players in the body's detoxification systems. Finally, both soluble and insoluble dietary fibers activate liver detoxification systems and can act as a natural "broom," sweeping toxins out of the body.

PROBIOTICS:

Probiotics were discussed in depth in the previous section for their numerous benefits to gastrointestinal and immune system health. Probiotics help decrease the growth of undesirable gut microbes, improve nutrient absorption, neutralize intestinal toxins, and produce substances that help heal the leaky gut. Probiotics are especially important during and after antibiotic use, but are best used on a regular basis throughout life. High dose probiotic supplementation may be used to help heal leaky gut, to decrease food hypersensitivities and to assist in the elimination of parasites and other undesirable gut microbes. They should always be used in conjunction with prebiotics, which are indigestible carbohydrates used as fuel by probiotic microbes. *Fructooligosaccharides, guar gum, cellulose, oat bran, and legume fiber* are some of the most potent prebiotics.

IDENTIFY:

People with brain-related problems often have persistent adverse food reactions that need to be identified and appropriately dealt with. This step should not be ignored or minimized. In my experience, identifying and properly managing food allergies or intolerances can bring about dramatic improvements in cognitive performance, behaviour and overall health. I have witnessed many lives completely turned around by the identification and management of food allergies or intolerances. However, because food related symptoms will often be diminished as the leaky gut heals, it is usually preferable to carry out the preceding steps (ANT P) for a while before trying to identify adverse food reactions. Effective methods for identification of food allergies and other adverse reactions to foods will be covered in the next chapter.

As well, identification of parasites and other unfriendly gut inhabitants can be an important step in gastrointestinal rehabilitation. I have found it quite amazing how many kids with brain-related difficulties have intestinal parasites. Identifying and then eliminating undesirable gut organisms can often bring about very clear benefits. Stool testing for parasites can be ordered by most healthcare professionals. Medical doctors can order this test but most will do so only if the patient has acute or persistent diarrhea. Nutritionally oriented medical doctors, and other natural healthcare providers such as naturopathic physicians, order these test more routinely. Testing for intestinal yeast overgrowth or the presence of other undesirable gut microbes may also be done.

ELIMINATE:

1. Allergic or intolerant foods.

Once allergic or intolerant foods have been identified, they should be carefully eliminated from the diet. Plenty of good recipes and food preparation principles are presented later in the recipe book to help make these changes as easy as possible. In many cases, if problematic foods are eliminated for a few months while the gut is being supported through proper nutrition and probiotics, these problematic foods can be gradually reintroduced and eaten again, at least on an infrequent basis. Junk foods, fast foods, rich desserts and over processed, devitalized foods should be permanently avoided as much as possible. Once the leaky gut has healed, many people can occasionally indulge in these kinds of foods without major setbacks.

2. Intestinal parasites or other undesirable gut microbes.

Parasites found in stool testing should usually be eliminated. Besides having the potential to cause or contribute to the leaky gut, parasites can "turn on" the immune system's allergic responsiveness and lead to worsening food allergies or intolerances. In the Western world, most parasites found on stool examination are single-celled animals known as protozoans. Medical doctors may prescribe anti-parasitic drugs to eliminate parasites but usually only for those with persistent abdominal pain or diarrhea who have confirmed infections of certain protozoan or worm parasites. Health food stores carry a variety of herbal remedies intended to cleanse the gut of parasites. Whatever approach is used, it is advisable to have the stool checked for parasites after the course of treatment is complete to confirm that parasites are indeed eliminated. Ongoing nutritional support of gut immune function and probiotic supplementation are the most effective ways to prevent re-establishment of gut parasites.

the war within:
food allergies and the brain

The Food Allergy Controversy

few things are as controversial among medical doctors as the assertion that various dissimilar medical complaints or health conditions are the result of food allergies. As a general rule, family doctors have a tendency to label hard-to-define complaints, with no apparent "cause," as psychosomatic illnesses. The idea that adverse food reactions might play a significant role in many of these complaints seems preposterous to most physicians. "A food allergy? Hah! Show me the hives, swollen lips or trouble breathing after eating food!" This is unfortunate for their patients.

True Food Allergy

Part of the reason for this controversy is that the term "allergy" refers to only a very narrow and well defined type of adverse reaction. Most laypeople will refer to any adverse food reactions as an "allergy," whereas most physicians only recognize a food allergy when it fits the strict definition of an allergy. An "allergy" is defined in medical texts as a very specific and well defined type of adverse reaction of the immune system to a specific molecule, usually a protein. Allergic reactions to food can happen after ingesting a very small amount of the offending substance. Allergic reactions usually occur immediately after exposure to food allergens. They are caused by the release of the chemical histamine, and other powerful chemicals, from specific immune cells. Depending upon where histamine is released, it can cause symptoms such as: hives; swollen or itchy lips, mouth and throat; breathing difficulties; itching eyes or a stuffy nose.

Food allergies can also cause abdominal pain, nausea or vomiting, and can vary from mild and barely detectable to severe anaphylaxis (severe swelling with difficulty breathing),which can even result in rapid death. In fact, no poison can kill you faster than your own immune system if you have a severe allergic (anaphylactic) reaction to food. Fortunately, only 1-5% of adults and 3-7% of children have clearly definable food allergies. Because allergic diseases are rapidly rising throughout society these percentages are increasing, but a true food allergy still only accounts for only a small percentage of all adverse food reactions.

Food Intolerances

A far higher percentage of people, perhaps as many as 75%, experience other adverse reactions to food. These can be classified as either food intolerances or food hypersensitivities. Food intolerances generally refer to non-immunological reactions to foods such as those that occur when food is improperly digested.

An increasingly common example is lactose intolerance, which causes abdominal pain, bloating and gas in those who cannot digest milk sugar. When you are "lactose intolerant," milk sugar ferments in the gut producing gas and irritating acids instead of being easily digested and absorbed. Food intolerances can also include adverse symptoms from the body's improper processing of natural or artificial food chemicals. An example of this would be the headaches and flushing experienced by people with intolerance to MSG. Of course food intolerance can also occur to some extent in anyone who overeats, especially if the foods they eat are heavy in fat, sugar or refined starches. (Just the way you feel after stuffing yourself with a holiday dinner).

These symptoms should also act as a warning. Stress on intestinal cells caused by intolerance reactions can increase intestinal permeability (cause leaky gut), especially if the food one is intolerant to is eaten on a regular basis. Leaky gut can occur temporarily after one big junk food binge, leaving a person feeling like 'death warmed over' for days. If bad eating habits persist, so will the leaky gut. Once leaky gut syndrome develops, you'll find that the list of foods that seem to cause adverse reactions grows and grows. It becomes more difficult to determine which foods are causing the problems as chronic symptoms persist from day to day.

Some of the most common chemicals in food that cause food intolerance reactions:

- Amines
- Benzoates
- BHA, BHT
- Excesses of any food (especially fat, sugar, salt or refined starches)
- Hydrogenated vegetable oils (trans fatty acids)
- Lactose
- MSG (Monosodium Glutamate)
- Nitrites
- Rancid or heat damaged fats
- Salicylates
- Sulfites
- Tartrazine

Food Hypersensitivities

Food allergies are also known as *immediate hypersensitivity* or Type I hypersensitivity reactions because they result in immediate and well-defined allergy symptoms such as hives, swollen lips or breathing difficulties. More common than true food allergies are *delayed hypersensitivity* reactions, also known as Type III hypersensitivity reactions. These adverse reactions occur primarily in people with increased intestinal permeability (leaky gut) and result when large quantities of antibodies are bound to food molecules that have passed through the leaky gut. The large molecules formed when antibodies attach to food molecules are known as immune complexes. Small amounts of immune complexes can be removed by specialized immune cells in the gut and liver. They probably cause no harm. However, if the number and size of immune complexes exceeds the clearance capacity of the immune cells in the gut and liver, they may trigger an inflammatory response by the immune system.

Inflammation is not your friend! It causes a wide range of unpleasant symptoms. Most people with delayed hypersensitivity reactions are unaware that they are reacting adversely to specific foods. Instead, they often suffer with a variety of vague complaints such as fatigue, anxiety and muscle pain. It is quite common for someone to crave the foods that are causing their adverse food reactions, and to

What are the Symptoms?

The following is a partial list of common symptoms or medical disorders associated with food allergies or other adverse reactions to food. Symptoms recognized by most allergy specialists as indicators of true food allergies are marked with an asterisk*.

Respiratory

Non-seasonal runny nose, nasal congestion
Allergic rhinitis (hay fever)
Allergic conjunctivitis (red, itchy eyes)
Recurrent serious otitis media*
   (inflammation and fluid in the
   middle ear)
Asthma/wheezing*
Throat swelling (in serious anaphylactic
   reactions)*

Skin Reactions

Eczema*
Hives*
Swelling of mouth, eyelids and lips
   (angioedema)*
Itching skin*
Flushed face or ears after eating

Brain and Nervous System

Dizziness
Irritability or aggression
Hyperactivity, agitation or anxiety
Poor concentration
Mental exhaustion
Insomnia
Migraine headache

Musculoskeletal

Muscle pain
Muscular weakness
Muscular tension
Twitching muscles
Joint aches
Joint stiffness

Digestion

Diarrhea*
Belly pain/cramping*
Constipation*
Nausea and/or vomiting*
Bloating*
Burping*
Flatulence*
Upset stomach or indigestion*

Miscellaneous

Persistent or recurring fatigue
Dark circles under eyes
Paleness
Excessive sweating, feverishness or chills
Rapid heartbeat
Bed wetting
Frequent urination and excessive thirst

Note: Symptoms may occur immediately after eating certain foods or may take up to 24 hours or more to manifest. Symptoms may occur occasionally, or they may be constantly present.

This depends upon many factors including:

- whether the adverse reaction is immediate (true allergy) or delayed (hypersensitivity or intolerance)
- the amount and frequency of food eaten
- the nutritional status of the individual
- the state of their gastrointestinal health
- other health problems such as chronic infection, accumulated environmental toxins, lack of exercise or emotional stress.

never recognize that some of their favourite foods are actually ruining their health!

Note: To avoid being too wordy, we will often use the term "food allergy" in this book to refer to allergy, intolerance and hypersensitivity reactions.

When Food is the "Bad Guy": Identifying and Handling Adverse Food Reactions

Rather than having a recognizable reaction to specific foods, people with unmanaged food allergies or intolerances may just feel unwell much of the time. Because of this they may never associate their problems to the offending foods. Even when a specific food ingredient threatens life, as in *anaphylaxis*, it often takes real detective work to unravel the food allergy mystery.

Adults with unmanaged food allergies or intolerances may feel unwell and not know why. Children with such problems may not be able to clearly communicate what they're feeling, let alone tell you which foods are causing their troubles. Kids with untreated food allergies, or intolerances, tend to feel poorly much of the time. Rather than telling you they feel bad they tend to misbehave, be sad or moody, restless or hyperactive, or they may seem lazy or lethargic. Children with untreated food allergies or intolerances usually have cognitive problems and difficulties at school – even if they are bright kids.

As mentioned earlier, food allergic individuals often crave the very foods they are allergic to. Like an alcoholic, the food allergic person may experience momentary pleasure from these foods because of stress chemicals, adrenaline, cortisol or endorphins may be released following the ingestion of that food. This connection between food allergy and addiction may be why it is often hard for people to eliminate certain foods from their diet. Food addictions are most often associated with dairy or wheat allergy/intolerance.

Finding the Culprit

One of the most effective ways to identify food allergies and intolerances, or hypersensitivities is to temporarily restrict the diet, eliminating the foods most likely to be associated with allergic or other adverse reactions. If tailored correctly and adhered to, an elimination test diet can show observable improvements in mood, cognitive performance, energy levels, physical symptoms and general wellbeing within 1 to 4 weeks. In children, improvements in behaviour, attitude, reading abilities and school performance are often clearly observed. Once such improvements have been recognized and have remained consistent, foods can be systematically reintroduced to the diet, one food type at a time, carefully noting any adverse reactions.

Identifying food allergies and intolerances requires an organized step-by-step approach with a significant commitment of time and patience, but the information acquired can be truly life changing.

STEP 1: Conducting and Noting the Results of Diagnostic Tests (optional)

You may want to see a naturopathic physician or a nutritionally oriented medical doctor and have food allergy testing done. There are no completely foolproof laboratory tests, but some of them can provide important clues to make it easier to locate the causes of adverse food reactions. Skin tests are of little value in helping to identify adverse food reactions. RAST is a blood test used to identify the presence of antibodies associated with true food allergies only. ELISA testing can identify both true food allergies and the far more common Type III hypersensitivity or delayed food hypersensitivities. Food allergy testing can be very expensive and it is not a substitute for a carefully followed elimination diet.

STEP 2: The Diet and Symptom Diary

The participant, or a parent, should complete a Diet and Symptom diary for one week using the form provided at the end of this chapter (pp. 98-99). Make copies of this document and use one of these forms each day to record pertinent information, including:

■ Every food and beverage consumed (including all ingredients of recipes and packaged foods), the approximate quantity, the time of day and the location of the meal or snack.

■ Any symptoms noted after each meal such as behavioural, mood, or cognitive problems; abdominal pain, nausea, diarrhea, or constipation; itching skin, hives, wheezing, coughing, stuffy nose, sneezing, or runny nose; joint or muscle pains, and headaches.

■ The quality of sleep each night and how the person feels in the morning.

■ Energy levels, sense of exhaustion.

■ Any strong food preferences, food habits or possible food addictions noted during this time.

At the end of this first week, review the diet and symptom diary sheets to look for clues that suggest which foods may be causing adverse effects. It is important for the subject or parent to become accustomed to keeping careful records of foods and symptoms. Many food allergies and intolerances will only be uncovered through the process of careful observation.

STEP 3: Formulate and Follow an Elimination Test Diet

This step requires temporary adherence to a special diet based primarily upon whole foods. It does not include junk foods or chemical additives. The test diet requires the elimination of:

- junk foods, processed foods, food additives
- all dairy products (including goat milk products)
- wheat, corn, baker's and brewer's yeast
- eggs
- peanuts and any peanut products
- soy
- chocolate
- orange and orange flavouring
- refined sugar

Other foods may also be eliminated if they are suggested by the diet and symptom diary or by allergy testing.

Guidelines for a standard elimination test diet are found at the end of this chapter with elimination test diet recipes and food preparation hints in the recipe section. The restrictions may seem overwhelming at first, but the recipes and hints found later in this book will make the process as easy and enjoyable as possible. Rather than thinking about this as a restrictive diet, you should consider this to be an interesting new eating adventure for your whole family.

It may take several weeks for some people to be able to follow their elimination test diet. In my experience it is far better for families to follow the elimination test diet together rather than placing special restrictions on one family member and having to prepare special meals for them.

The first week on this diet is often the most difficult. In fact, many people feel or behave worse than they did before the diet during these first few days. In some ways this can be likened to an addict in withdrawal. Fortunately, this withdrawal period will soon pass as the benefits of the restricted diet become apparent. By the end of the second week many children and adults feel better than they have at any other time in their lives. It really IS worth the effort.

STEP 4: The Food Challenge Process

This step involves identification of allergic or intolerant foods by a careful and systematic reintroduction method known as the food challenge process. Once the child or adult has been carefully following an elimination test diet for two to four weeks, food challenges can begin.

The order of food challenges is not important as long as all foods that were eliminated are eventually reintroduced and tested. Most commonly, dairy and wheat are the first foods to be challenged, since they are the most common foods to cause adverse food reactions. Test only one food on one particular day. The challenged food is generally eaten at breakfast, lunch and supper, doubling the quantity eaten with each meal. For example, milk might be challenged by drinking 1/2 glass for breakfast, 1 glass for lunch and 2 glasses for supper. If a clear adverse reaction to the challenged food occurs, it is not necessary to challenge it again at subsequent meals.

The participant or parent must keep careful records of the foods eaten, the quantity consumed, the time of day and any symptoms experienced after eating these foods. A special Food Challenge Diary form is included for your use at the end of this chapter (pp. 100-101). Copy this document and use one form for each food challenge.

Food challenges occur on one day and symptoms are observed that day as well as the following day. Any physical symptoms, bad behaviours, mood swings or cognitive problems experienced by the subject during the day are recorded, along with the time the symptoms occur. The participant or parent should also record the quality of sleep that night and how

Be sure to make enough copies of the Food Challenge Diary Form to be able to carry out all necessary food challenges. A typical food challenge schedule might go something like this:

Day 1   challenge dairy (e.g. milk, cheese; breakfast, lunch, supper)

Day 2   back to elimination test diet

Day 3   challenge wheat (wheat without yeast, e.g. wheat crisp bread (no yeast) or puffed wheat alone or with rice milk; breakfast, lunch, supper)

Day 4   back to elimination test diet

Day 5   challenge corn (e.g. corn chips, corn meal, popcorn; breakfast, lunch, supper)

Day 6   back to elimination test diet

Day 7   challenge eggs (e.g. boiled, fried (no butter), scrambled (no milk added, no bread); breakfast, lunch, supper)

Day 8   back to elimination test diet

Day 9   challenge peanuts (e.g. peanut butter, roasted in shell; breakfast, lunch, supper)

Day 10   back to elimination test diet

Day 11   challenge soy (e.g. soymilk, tofu, roasted soy nuts, soy yogurt; breakfast, lunch, supper)

Day 12   back to elimination test diet

Day 13   challenge chocolate (may use pure chocolate bar for this challenge; breakfast, lunch, supper)

Day 14   back to elimination test diet

Day 15   challenge oranges (breakfast, lunch, supper)

Day 16   back to elimination test diet

Day 17   challenge sugar (e.g. use pure table sugar in food or use sugar cubes to suck on; breakfast, lunch, supper)

            End of Food Challenge Process (Note: Food additives may also be challenged, but this is complex and may require professional guidance)

NOTE: In addition, before eating the test food, the participant should sit quietly and measure his or her pulse rate (in heartbeats per minute). This information should be recorded on the Food Challenge Diary form. After the challenge food is eaten, the participant should remain still and measure the pulse rate after five minutes and then after ten minutes. Record the pulse rates on the form provided (Food Challenge Diary pg 100). If the pulse rate rises 15 beats or more from the resting rate, this may be a stress response indicating an adverse food reaction.

the participant feels and behaves the next day. Fatigue, bad breath, stuffy nose, headaches, moodiness, aggressiveness or other bad behaviours the day after a food challenge should all be recorded. If the participant gets sick with a cold or ear infection following a food challenge, this should be noted and further challenges should not occur until the participant has fully recovered from the infection.

Food allergies or intolerances may cause the release of the stress hormone adrenaline, which usually pumps up the pulse rate by about ten beats per minute or more. Such a rise will help confirm the presence of an adverse food reaction.

Remember that once challenged, a food must be completely withdrawn again until all foods are challenged, even if no adverse effects are noted from the food. Also, allow at least a full day without food challenges to elapse before another food challenge is done. This is important for accurate observation and recording.

For older children or adolescents it is also worthwhile to challenge junk foods by letting the adolescent binge on junk foods during one of the challenge days. This will let them experience how dreadful they feel after eating these foods and may help them to understand why they should avoid them. Be sure to have adolescents record how they feel after their junk food binge, in case they are tempted to start eating junk food again.

Challenge Yourself to the Food Challenge - And Win

Obviously, the food challenge process is a lengthy task, which requires a high level of commitment on the part of the participant and any other supportive family member. Unfortunately, I know of no better way to accurately determine and help eliminate food allergies and intolerances. Some of the most renowned food allergy clinics in the world rely exclusively on this method.

STEP 5: Putting it all Together

Now it's time to create a long-term diet plan based on the results of the previous steps. Once the allergic and intolerant foods have been identified with a high level of confidence, it is important to remain watchful for adverse food reactions on an ongoing basis. For instance, if your child has a particularly bad day in terms of behaviour and mood, it is well worthwhile to recollect the foods that were eaten over the past few days. Make a record of these foods and if adverse reactions to these foods are noted to cause problems repeatedly, steps should be taken to avoid them. Many people will find that their child has an especially difficult time after events like holidays, birthdays, visits to fast food restaurants or other junk food binges. Eventually, you and your child may both decide that the few moments of pleasure are not worth the suffering!

As time goes on, adverse food reactions can evolve and change. Particularly, children's responses to foods can change. Many outgrow some of their food allergies or intolerances and following the "ANT PIE" program can heal a leaky gut and improve immune function. Over the weeks or months, positive dietary changes can reduce sensitivities to previously difficult foods to the point where it may be possible to eat them again in small quantities without ill effects. However, avoiding junk food and sticking with a diet rich in whole foods, fruits, vegetables and whole grains is a lifelong commitment to good health. It's a commitment each of us should make, especially those with ADHD, chronic fatigue syndrome or other chronic conditions.

The prize? A healthy brain, a healthy body and a new positive outlook on life.

the standard elimination test diet

The elimination test diet continues for 4-8 weeks and then, if results are positive, changes are noted.

Foods to Avoid:

Dairy

- any type of milk, or dairy products including cheeses, ice cream, and cream cheese. Goat's milk or products made from goat's milk are not suitable substitutes. Goat's milk is almost equal to cow's milk for allergic potential.
- products that have casein, lactose, and whey on the label.
- limit butter use. Alternatives to butter are oils or ghee. (See butter alternatives on page 146).

Wheat

- all wheat pastas, spaghetti and breads.

- durham, semolina, whole wheat, white breads or flours. "Flour" on a label usually means wheat.
- kamut, (similar to wheat). It may be tolerated later even by those intolerant to wheat, but may not be used while on the elimination test diet.
- products that have gluten or gliaden on the label.

Corn

- all corn, corn meal, corn chips, cornstarch and other products containing corn.

Yeast (brewer's and baker's)

- all yeast breads, cookies and cakes, including sourdough and naturally risen breads (these contain naturally occurring yeasts).
- yeast or yeast extract in prepared foods.
- salad dressings and packaged soups containing yeast. Read labels.

NOTE: *small amounts of Red Star nutritional yeast are generally acceptable (less than 1 teaspoon per meal).*

Eggs

- eggs, egg whites and egg yolks and any products with eggs in them.
- cookies, cakes and breads that have eggs in them.
- other products with eggs, egg whites and lactalbumin on the label.

Peanuts

- whole peanuts, peanut butter.

Soy

- all non-fermented soy products: soybeans, soymilk, tofu, margarine, and soybean oil.
- products with soy protein isolate, texturized vegetable protein (TVP), or any type of soy on the label. Read labels carefully, many products contain soy.

NOTE: Small amounts (less than 1 tablespoon per meal of the following fermented soy products are acceptable: preservative and wheat free soy sauce (Tamari), miso, tempeh.

Chocolate

- cocoa products, chocolate bars, chips, cookies and cakes.
- products with cocoa, cocoa beans or chocolate on the label.

Oranges

- whole oranges, orange juice and orange flavouring.
- Check all juice labels for oranges, orange juice concentrate and added sugars.

Sugar

- all refined white sugar (sucrose).
- products with added sugar, glucose, corn syrup and sucrose on the label.
- pure fructose (in small quantities) is generally acceptable. It is a low-allergy potential, low glycemic index sweetener.

Food Additives

- added artificial preservatives, flavourings and colourings including:
  Sodium benzoate, sulfites, nitrates, BHA, BHT, artificial sweeteners such as aspartame or Nutrasweet, yellow dye #5, tartrazine, or other dyes, monosodium glutamate or MSG.
- Jell-O®, Kool-aid®, fruit punch and all beverages containing sugar or artificial flavours or sweeteners, cereals with preservatives and added sugars, packaged foods containing these additives. **Read labels**.

Oils/Fats

- trans-fatty acids (hydrogenated or partially-hydrogenated oils, vegetable oil shortening). Check labels of cookies, crackers, cakes, and chips! Most of these foods contain hydrogenated oils.
- margarine and products containing margarine.
- vegetable oil shortening, which is mostly hydrogenated vegetable oil.
- all oil fried or deep fried foods.

Beverages

- coffee or alcoholic beverages. (Small amounts of black or green tea and unlimited herbal teas allowed).
- sugary drinks including juices.

NOTE: Unsweetened juices are acceptable in small amounts (less than 1 cup per day total) if they are diluted with twice as much water as called for on can. Purified water is the preferred beverage.

Foods You May Eat:

Cereal

- cream of rice, oatmeal, or any hot cereals which do not contain wheat or corn.
- puffed rice, puffed millet, acceptable packaged cold cereals with no wheat, added sugar or additives can be found at health food stores.

Grains

- rice: preferably brown, brown basmati, jasmine, rice pasta, plain rice cakes, rice bread.
- wheat free/yeast free flat breads and rye crisps, millet, quinoa, amaranth, teff, oats, barley, rye.

Flours

- rice, millet, quinoa, amaranth, teff, bean flours, oat, barley, and rye.

Fruits

- all EXCEPT oranges; preferably fresh.
- organic is best!
- dried fruit should be free of sulfites.

Vegetables

- all vegetables, eat lots! Fresh and organic are best.

Protein

- all types of meats are acceptable, except processed meats including cold cuts, hams and wieners.
- all poultry is acceptable (free range is best).

- all ocean water fish are acceptable. Try to include salmon, sardines, occasional tuna and halibut.
- beans and legumes: you can have all beans and legumes you want EXCEPT peanuts and soy products. Check labels of canned beans, dips, and soups for sweeteners and additives.
- nuts: cashews, pistachios, almonds, brazil nuts, walnuts, pine nuts; all nuts are acceptable EXCEPT peanuts, soy nuts, roasted and salted nuts. Use nut butters such as almond butter or cashew butter. Great for sauces, salad dressings, and butter/peanut butter alternatives.
- seeds: All are acceptable and encouraged. Sunflower seeds and pumpkin seeds are great. Tahini, a sesame seed butter, is great for dressings and sauces!

Oils/Fats

- olive, canola, sunflower, safflower, sesame, flax or coconut oil.
- ghee is clarified butter and is acceptable on this diet. Great for sautés. Method for making ghee is in recipe section on page 218.
- coconut oil is the most stable oil for cooking (use for light sautés).

*NOTE: Store flaxseed oil in a dark bottle in the refrigerator and use as dressing or in smoothies; **do not heat flaxseed oil.***

Sweeteners

- in general, use sparingly.
- acceptable sweeteners include: molasses (unsulfured), pure maple syrup, honey, stevia (herbal sweetener you can get at natural food stores, very sweet so use very small amounts), brown rice syrup, pure fructose, Lo Han Kuo

extract (very sweet extract from Chinese fruit), agave syrup (natural fructose).

Beverages

- drink lots of water! Filtered water or bottled spring water is best.
- herbal teas including green tea, jasmine, chamomile and Oolong (read labels). Kids can learn to enjoy herbal tea including small amounts of green tea. **See tea recipes pages 250-252.**
- fresh vegetable juices are great! Kids can learn to love carrot juice (Especially when mixed with apple juice).
- rice milk.
- all fruit juice EXCEPT orange juice. Use fruit juice sparingly and dilute with twice the recommended quantity of water. Maximum 1 cup per day total.

NOTE: NO juice, tea, or soft drinks with added corn syrup, sugar, glucose, or colourings.

Condiments

- salt, pepper, garlic, lemon, fresh parsley, chives and other herbs.
- all natural spices are permitted. Seasoning salts often contain added sugar or MSG - check labels carefully.
- Spike®, a natural seasoning salt blend, is very tasty and nutritious (contains a small amount of nutritional yeast which is OK in very small amounts).
- vanilla (pure), unsweetened carob, baking powder with NO aluminum, baking soda.
- wheat free, preservative free Tamari soy sauce and miso are acceptable in small amounts. **See pages 211-222 for condiment recipes and suggestions.**

Diet and Symptom Diary
Please photocopy for your use.

TIME OF DAY & LOCATION	FOOD & BEVERAGES Every food and beverage consumed (including all ingredients for recipes and packaged foods), the approximate quantity of each.	FOOD BEHAVIOURS Any strong food preferences, food habits or possible food addictions noted during this time.
Time .... Location		
Time .... Location		
Time .... Location		

Overall, today was: ☐ Good ☐ Fair ☐ Poor ☐ Terrible

Comments:...

Quality of sleep following this day was: ☐ Good ☐ Fair ☐ Poor ☐ Terrible

For (participant) _____ Date: _____

SYMPTOMS

Any symptoms noted after each meal such as behaviourial, mood or cognitive problems; hyperactivity; exhaustion; abdominal pain, nausea, diarrhea or constipation; itching skin, hives, wheezing, coughing, stuffy nose, sneezing or runny nose; joint or muscle pains and headaches.

Record any symptoms noted from the time the food is eaten until the next meal.

....

....

....

....

....

....

Record any symptoms noted from the time the food is eaten until the next meal.

....

....

....

....

....

....

Record any symptoms noted from the time the food is eaten **until the end of the next day**.

....

....

....

....

....

....

Food Challenge Diary

Please photocopy for your use.

TIME OF DAY & LOCATION		FOOD & BEVERAGES Describe the exact type of food challenged and the quantity consumed	PULSE RATE Before and after food challenge. Record pulse rate at wrist in beats per minute (BPM). Keep still until you are finished taking measurements.
Breakfast	(Single serving of challenge food)	Food (only challenge 1 type of food on any given day)	Before challenge: [ ] (BPM) 5 minutes after: [ ] (BPM) 10 minutes after: [ ] (BPM)
Lunch	(Two servings of challenge food)	Food (only challenge 1 type of food on any given day)	Before challenge: [ ] (BPM) 5 minutes after: [ ] (BPM) 10 minutes after: [ ] (BPM)
Dinner	(Three servings of challenge food)	Food (only challenge 1 type of food on any given day)	Before challenge: [ ] (BPM) 5 minutes after: [ ] (BPM) 10 minutes after: [ ] (BPM)

Overall, today was: ☐ Good ☐ Fair ☐ Poor ☐ Terrible

Comments:..

Quality of sleep following this day was: ☐ Good ☐ Fair ☐ Poor ☐ Terrible

For (participant) _____ Date: _____

SYMPTOMS

Any symptoms noted after each meal such as behavioural, mood or cognitive problems; hyperactivity; exhaustion; abdominal pain, nausea, diarrhea or constipation; itching skin, hives, wheezing, coughing, stuffy nose, sneezing or runny nose; joint or muscle pains and headaches.

Record any symptoms noted from the time the food is eaten until the next meal.

....
....
....
....
....
....

Record any symptoms noted from the time the food is eaten until the next meal.

....
....
....
....
....
....

Record any symptoms noted from the time the food is eaten **until the end of the next day**.

....
....
....
....
....
....

Behaviour/health the day after food challenge: ☐ Good ☐ Fair

☐ Poor ☐ Terrible

Comments:...

smart nutrition
in a nutshell

the purpose of the previous chapters has been to lay a foundation, explaining the many nutritional factors that influence brain function. In this chapter I want to summarize for quick and easy reference so this program will be as practical and easy as possible for you or your child. This chapter organizes and simplifies the program into its most basic elements, and is meant to serve as a bridge to the food and recipes section where you'll find recipes, hints and food preparation guides to make these dietary changes a reality.

Treat Your Brain Cells Right!

Brain cells are very sensitive to toxic stresses. Junk foods, snack foods, fast foods and other chemically laden processed foods are all prime sources of toxic stress on the brain. Deep fried fats and hydrogenated vegetable oils are some of the most dangerous to the brain. Pesticide-contaminated food and genetically modified organisms are also potentially damaging to brain cells and should be avoided by choosing organic foods whenever possible.

Fueling the Human Supercomputer

An optimum diet for the brain, and overall health, is based on a balanced foundation of whole, natural foods: whole grains, fruits and vegetables, dairy or other calcium sources, meat or other good sources of protein and healthy oils. To support optimal brain function, the diet should be richly supplied with brain-critical nutrients including:

■ **Essential fatty acids: especially the omega 3 fatty acid DHA and the omega 6 fatty acid GLA.** Products such as Learning Factors School Aid by Natural Factors are an abundant and pollutant-free source of these brain critical fatty acids.

■ **Other brain critical nutrients: low-allergy potential protein, iron, calcium, magnesium, zinc, other trace elements, B vitamins, brain protective antioxidants, phytochemicals, and nutrients** to support effective toxin elimination. Learning Factors Smoothie Mix is a comprehensive product that combines all of these brain critical nutrients in a food powder that can be used to make delicious smoothies. It is designed to be used in combination with Learning Factors School Aid essential fatty acid supplements.

Revitalize the Gut-Brain Connection

Sub-optimal brain function is often associated with disturbances in the structure, function and microscopic ecology of the gastrointestinal tract. *Leaky gut syndrome* is a common condition resulting from chronic irritation of, or poor nutritional support for, the normally leakproof lining of the small intestine. When the small intestine becomes leaky, large, partially digested food particles and byproducts of microorganisms passively leak through the intestine, putting a great deal of stress upon the immune system and liver. The result can be a variety of symptoms including food intolerances, malaise, poor concentration, irritability, fatigue, and muscle pain. When beneficial intestinal bacteria (probiotics) diminish and are replaced by microscopic parasites or unfriendly bacteria or yeasts, stress upon the gut, immune system and brain are the inevitable result.

To heal a leaky gut and restore normal microbiological ecology to the intestinal tract, a step-by-step process is followed. My way to remember it is with an acronym of the first letters: ANT PIE.

- **A**bstain from gut stressful foods, bad habits, drugs, chemicals in foods and overeating.
- **N**ourish the gut and immune system with supportive nutrients.
- **T**oxins: support the body's natural detoxification processes through specific nutrients.
- **P**robiotics: use proven strains with prebiotics (dietary fiber that supports probiotic growth)
- **I**dentify food allergies/intolerances, gut parasites and other unfriendly microbes.
- **E**liminate gut parasites and other unfriendly microbes, allergenic/intolerant foods, toxic burdens through an effective detoxification program.

The "ANT P" part of this program is straightforward. Learning Factors Smoothie Mix along with Learning Factors School Aid essential fatty acid supplements are designed to support gastrointestinal revitalization. These two supplements alone provide support for much of the "ANT PIE" program. Natural Factors also manufactures some of the most effective probiotic supplements available. Look for the Natural Factors supplements that contain the bacteria *Lactobacillus rhamnosus* and Propio-Fidus™, These friendly bacteria should always be part of any effective gastrointestinal rehabilitation program.

Identifying and dealing with food allergies/intolerances is the subject of Chapter 8 of this book. Food allergies are relatively uncommon compared to other types of adverse reactions to foods. Adverse food reactions can place a great deal of stress upon the immune system and interfere with brain function. In many cases, identifying and eliminating certain foods can result in profound improvements in mood, cognitive performance and behaviour. The identification

Brain Critical Nutrition Made Simple

Learning Factors School Aid - Essential Fatty Acid Supplement*

First 3 months
Long term maintenance

*1 teaspoon of the Learning Factors School Aid essential fatty acid liquid supplement is equivalent to 4 capsules of the Learning Factors School Aid in soft gel capsules.

Learning Factors School Aid

2-6 Years
4-6 capsules per day

7-12 Years
6-8 capsules per day

12 and up
8-10 capsules per day

Learning Factors Smoothie Mix

2-6 Years
1 - 1 1/2 scoop per day

7-12 Years
2 - 3 scoops per day

12 and up
3 - 5 scoops per day

of food allergies and other reactions to foods primarily involves a diet in which junk foods and commonly allergenic/intolerant foods are eliminated. This diet continues for 1 to 3 weeks and the individuals behaviour, mood, school performance and overall health is observed. Following this, foods are reintroduced one at a time and the effects of these reintroductions are carefully recorded on the form provided in Chapter 8. After all questionable foods are challenged, the worst offenders can be removed from the diet.

Identifying gut parasites and other unfriendly microbes, along with eliminating these unwelcome invaders is best done under the care of a nutritionally oriented healthcare practitioner and it is beyond the scope of this book. Eliminating body burdens of brain stressful toxins is the subject of other written materials available through your local health food store.

section two

the smart nutrition program
preparing smart food for a healthy brain

FOOD FOR THOUGHT

"Fast food not only comes with poisons inside the food, and with the destruction of the environment, but also with its own set of values, which is that food isn't important: It's cheap, you can eat it fast, and you don't have to eat with your kids."

Alice Waters, 2001

part I:
getting ready

The purpose of Section Two of this book is two-fold

1 To help you become both psychologically ready and practically organized for the Elimination Test Diet, and

2 To provide you with a selection of diverse nutritious recipes and sample menus which will serve as the basis for healthy, delicious, and low-allergy potential eating patterns for you and your entire family.

As you prepare for this new journey, try to keep in mind that this is not about "going on a diet," but rather becoming more conscious of how the food choices you make positively or negatively affect your brain and your body – your entire well-being. While it is true that changing established eating habits can present emotional and time-management challenges to a North American food culture which has become accustomed to eating fast food on the run, this is not another diet you have to survive, but one to help you re-energize and thrive!

Once you learn to fuel your brain and body for maximum health and vitality, you will rid yourself of allergies and intolerances, improve energy and stamina, prevent chronic disease, become more attuned to your body and its unique needs, as well as develop an increased awareness of nature's incredible seasonal cornucopia of food and your enlivened and enriched palate!

NOTE: Once you have completed the elimination test diet described in Chapter 8 and have determined your allergic or intolerant foods, you may be able to add back dairy, wheat or other foods not allowed on the elimination test diet. This book provides only recipes consistent with the elimination test diet, so you will have to find recipes that include non-elimination test diet foods in other cook books.

Food IQ Information

Packaged, so-called convenient, fast foods are damaging to our brain chemistry. They provide very few of the essential fats that feed our brains. Instead, they contain huge amounts of saturated fat, sugar and sodium in excess of what our bodies can handle. They contain only minute amounts of B and C vitamins or essential minerals and fiber. A typical 4 oz fast food burger can contain up to 690 mg of sodium, 20 g of fat (of which 8 g is saturated), and only 2 g of fiber. Add the ketchup and mayonnaise for more fat and more sugar. Behavioural symptoms of too much fat, sodium or sugar are irritability, restlessness, and lethargy.

Part 1 Getting Ready

Part 2 Tips for Preparing Food and Planning Menus

Part 3 The Recipes

Shop, Stop,
Read Labels, and Stock!

*"The decisions you make at a grocery store, at a restaurant, and
in your own kitchen have an importance that is often overlooked:
They help to determine the quality and nature of the life that
will be yours thereafter. Every time you shop, every time you prepare
food and every time you sit down to eat, you have
an opportunity to say "Yes!" to a healthier you."*

John Robbins, 1992

Shopping for the Elimination Test Diet

Getting ready to shop for the Elimination Test Diet requires some preparation: a little detective work, the information provided in the charts on the pages to follow, and knowing what your food budget can handle.

First, you will need to:

- Get to know your community natural health food store if there is one in your area. Call ahead to ask about the availability of what you need to buy. Ask if it's possible to have "an elimination test diet products tour" of the store with a knowledgeable store employee.
- Inform yourself as to what's available at your community supermarket. Depending on where you live, many supermarkets now offer a natural/organic foods section in the produce areas, alternative grain breads in the bakery section, healthful snacks and organic juices, and a variety of non-dairy alternatives. Ask customer service for assistance in finding what you need.
- Check out the local farmers' markets or food stands in your area. Local farmers' produce is fresh and in season. Many offer organic, or transitional organic, pesticide-free fruits and vegetables, free-range eggs and chickens, and organic, hormone-free beef and pork.

Secondly, before heading out:

- You may want to take along a small notebook as your "passport guide" through health food stores, supermarkets, and your local farmers' markets.

■ Each time you shop, you will want to include in your notebook: the charts of the Foods Allowed, ETD Pantry and Refrigerator charts, the List of Foods and Food Additives to Avoid, and the ingredients for your personal Weekly Menu Plan (see pages 256-257). Also keep a copy of these charts inside your pantry door and on your refrigerator. Take note of where you find the required foods and ingredients and the best buys for your money. Eventually, you will acquire a handy list of your favourite recipes and their ingredients.

Thirdly, allow more for your food budget

■ Because you will have to replace many of the staples in your fridge and pantry, your first trip will be your costliest. While we encourage buying organic, pesticide-free produce whenever possible, as well as expeller pressed cooking oils, you will have to make the decisions which best suit your personal or family budgets. Eventually, you will find where you can find the best deals, and realize that eliminating expensive, packaged, processed, and prepared convenience foods will cut down on your costs. Your new approach to eating will lead to improved health and vitality and also likely reduce spending on medications.

Food Additives to Avoid

Artificial preservatives, flavourings, and colourings including:

- Sodium benzoate
- Sulfites
- Nitrates
- BHA
- BHT
- Artificial sweeteners such as aspartame or Nutrasweet

- Yellow dye #5
- Tartrazine or other dyes
- Monosodium glutamate or MSG
- Avoid Jell-O®, Kool-Aid®, fruit punch and all beverages containing sugar or artificial flavours or sweeteners
- Cereals with preservatives and added table sugar or sucrose
- Packaged foods containing the above additives.

Foods to Avoid

Dairy:

- Any type of milk or dairy products including cheeses, ice cream, and cream cheese.
- Avoid products that have casein, lactose, and whey on the label.
- Limit butter use. Alternatives to butter are oils or clarified butter.
- Goat's milk or products made from goat's milk are not suitable substitutes.

Wheat:

- All wheat pastas, spaghettis, and breads.
- Durham, semolina, whole wheat, white breads or flours. "Flour" on a label usually means wheat.
- Kamut (similar to wheat). This may prove to be well tolerated later even by those intolerant to wheat but may not be used while on the elimination test diet.
- Avoid products that have gluten or gliaden on the label.

Corn:

- All corn, corn meal, corn chips, cornstarch and other products containing corn.

Yeast:

- All yeast breads, cookies and cakes including sourdough and naturally risen breads (these may contain naturally occurring yeasts).
- Read labels for yeast or yeast extract in prepared foods.
- Many salad dressings and packaged soups contain yeast. Read labels.
  Note: Small amounts of Red Star® nutritional yeast are generally acceptable (less than 1 tsp. per meal)

Eggs:

- All eggs, egg whites, and egg yolks, and any products with eggs in them.
- Many cookies, cakes, and breads have eggs in them. Be sure to avoid them.
- Avoid products with eggs, egg whites and lactalbumin on the label.

Peanuts:

- Whole peanuts, peanut butter.

Soy:

- All non-fermented soy products: soybeans, soymilk, tofu, margarine, and soybean oil, (organic wheat-free tamari may be used sparingly).
- Avoid products with soy protein isolate, texturized vegetable protein (TVP), or any type of soy on the label.
  Note: Small amounts (less than 1 Tbsp per meal of the following fermented soy products are acceptable: preservative and wheat free soy sauce (Tamari), miso)

Chocolate:

- All cocoa products, cocoa bars, chocolate chips, cookies, and cakes.

Orange:

- Whole oranges, orange juice, orange juice concentrate, and orange flavouring.

Sugar:

- All refined white sugar (sucrose).
- Avoid products with added sugar, glucose, and corn syrup and sucrose on the label. Check all labels, especially juice and salad dressings.
- Pure fructose (in small quantities) is generally acceptable. It is a low-allergy potential, low glycemic index sweetener.

Oils/Fats:

- All trans-fatty acids (hydrogenated or partially-hydrogenated oils, vegetable oil shortening).
- Check all labels of cookies, crackers, cakes, and chips! Most of these contain hydrogenated oils.
- Margarine and products containing margarine, and vegetable oil shortening which is mostly hydrogenated vegetable oil.
- All oil fried or deep fried foods.

Beverages:

- Coffee or alcoholic beverages.
- Sugary drinks including juices.
- Unsweetened juices are acceptable in small amounts if they are diluted with twice as much water as called for on can.
- Purified water is the preferred beverage.

Food Additives:

- All artificial flavourings, colourings and preservatives including: sodium benzoate, sulfites, nitrates, BHA, BHT, asparteme, monosodium glutamate.

Foods Allowed

Cereal:

- Hot: Cream of rice, oatmeal, or any hot cereals which do not contain wheat or corn.
- Cold: Puffed rice, puffed millet, granola or muesli, acceptable packaged cold cereals with no wheat added, sugar or additives. Such cereals can be found at health food stores.

Grains:

- Rice: preferably brown, brown basmati, jasmine, rice pasta, plain rice cakes, rice bread.
- Wheat free/yeast free flat breads and rye crisps; millet, quinoa, amaranth, teff, oats, barley, rye.

Flours:

- Rice, millet, quinoa, amaranth, teff, bean flours, oat, barley, and rye.

Vegetables:

- All vegetables, eat lots! Fresh and organic if possible.

Protein:

- Meat: All types are acceptable, except all processed meats including cold cuts, hams and wieners.
- Poultry: All types are acceptable. (Free-range is best)
- Fish: All ocean water types are acceptable. Try to include salmon, sardines, occasional tuna, and halibut.
- Beans/Legumes: You can have all beans and legumes EXCEPT peanuts and soy products.

Check labels of canned beans, dips, and soups for sweeteners and additives.

- Nuts: Cashews, pistachios, almonds, brazil nuts, walnuts, pine nuts.

All nuts are acceptable EXCEPT peanuts, soy nuts, and all roasted and salted nuts.

Use nut butters (almond or cashew) NO PEANUT BUTTER!

- Seeds: All are acceptable and encouraged.
- Sunflower and pumpkin seeds are great. Tahini (sesame seed butter) is great.

Oils/Fats:

- Olive, sunflower, safflower, sesame, flax* or coconut oil.
- Clarified butter is acceptable on this diet and is great for sauté.
- Coconut oil is the most stable oil for cooking (use for light sautés).
- *Store flax oil in a dark bottle in the refrigerator and use as dressing or in smoothies. **DO NOT HEAT THIS OIL.**

Sweeteners:

In general, use sparingly.

- Acceptable sweeteners include molasses (unsulfured), pure maple syrup, honey, stevia, (herbal sweetener you can get at natural food store, very sweet so use a very small amount), Sucanat, brown rice syrup, pure fructose, agave syrup (natural fructose)

Beverages:

- Water: Filtered, reverse osmosis (RO) water is best.
- Herbal Teas: Green tea, jasmine, chamomile and oolong.
- Rice milk.
- All juice EXCEPT orange. Use fruit juice sparingly and dilute with twice the recommended quantity of water.
- NO juice, tea, or soft drinks with added corn syrup, sugar, glucose, or colourings.
- Kids can learn to enjoy herbal tea including small amounts of green tea.
- Fresh vegetable juices. Kids can learn to drink carrot juice.

Condiments:

- Salt, pepper, garlic, lemon, fresh parsley, chives, and other herbs.
- All natural spices are permitted.
- Spike® is very tasty and nutritious (contains small amounts of nutritional yeast which is ok).
- Vanilla extract (pure), unsweetened carob, baking powder with NO aluminum, baking soda.
- Wheat free, preservative free Tamari soy sauce and miso are acceptable in small amounts.

Re-stocking the Pantry and the Fridge for the Elimination Test Diet

Shopping and re-stocking for the Elimination Test Diet first require taking an inventory of what's in your pantry and fridge – a basic accounting of your current eating habits. For the duration of the Elimination Test Diet, you may find you will have to remove all the things that are *not* on your Foods Allowed List. Doing so will help you keep your life more simple, reduce possible temptations, and clean out the expired and wilting items in your pantry and fridge!

All oils (with the exception of olive oil and coconut oil) are stored in the refrigerator to prevent the oils from becoming rancid. The same is true of all flours, nuts and seeds, which need to be protected from rancidity. Whenever possible, store flours and any left-over food in recycled glass jars or glass containers. Otherwise, harmful industrial chemicals such as polyvinyl chlorides (PVCs) in plastic containers and plastic wrap can leach into the food and ultimately into you!

As you progress through the Elimination Test Diet and discover the foods to which you are allergic or intolerant, you will also determine which foods do not negatively affect you. This discovery will free you to add greater variety back into your pantry and refrigerator, and your daily fare.

The list below provides you with the staples for the Elimination Test Diet as well as the basis for a future pattern of mindful and nutritious eating habits. You may find it useful to include this list in your shopping notebook and keep one inside your pantry door. Included are most of the items you will need to make the recipes in this book. Keeping these products in stock will make for easier and more creative menu planning without having to run out and shop. Although there are many variations on these products, we have tried to keep things simple by using the same products throughout the recipe selections. We also suggest some reliable and readily available brands which may assist you when shopping.

The Elimination Test Diet Pantry

Grains:

Purchase organically grown grains whenever possible.
- Barley
- Buckwheat
- Oats
- Oat bran and rice bran
- Rice (basmati, brown, wild, white)

Quick cereals:

- Nature's Path Cold Cereal Eco Pacs: puffed rice, puffed millet, amaranth, quinoa, spelt
- Quick cooking oatmeal, kasha (buckwheat), cream of rice (whole grains), tapioca
- Nature's Path Organic Instant Hot Oatmeal in various flavours

Smoothies:

- Learning Factors Smoothie Mix. Naturally fruit flavoured and naturally sweetened or unflavoured, unsweetened. Additional ingredients required for smoothies include: Fruit (frozen is best); buy frozen or buy fresh when in season or on sale. Wash the fresh fruit, cut it up and put in on a cookie sheet. Freeze on cookie sheet and then put into freezer in ziplock freezer bags. Bananas can be peeled fresh, place directly into a bag and frozen. Grapes and berries can be washed and frozen without cutting up.

- Oil (flaxseed oil or Learning Factors School Aid spoonable oil)
- Green food powder (optional)
- Juice (unfiltered organic apple cider is very good) or Stevia for added sweetness.

Beans:

- Chick peas
- Black turtle beans
- Split Peas (green, yellow)
- Red kidney beans
- Lentils (red, brown)

Baking Essentials:

- Aluminum-free and sodium-free baking powder (available at health food stores), or make your own. (See page 139)
- Arrowroot powder (to replace cornstarch as a thickener for desserts, soups and sauces)
- Gelatin
- Agar-agar (a natural gelling agent for vegetarians as it is made from seaweed, and is high in fiber and vitamins and minerals)
- Egg Replacer (available at health food stores). Should not contain egg white or corn or wheat starch). EnergG® Egg Replacer is a brand available which is suitable for the Elimination Test Diet.
- Make your own Egg Replacer (See page 137)
- Spectrum Shortening® is a low-allergy potential product which works well for baking, especially pie crusts

Flours:

- Amaranth flour
- Barley flour

- Buckwheat flower
- Bulgur
- Chick-pea flour
- Tapioca flour
- Quinoa flour
- Rice flour
- Rye flour
- Spelt flour (if not sensitive to wheat)
- Oat flour (Quinoa flour, and Teff flour are also options)

Pasta:

- Rice noodles, arrowroot noodles, Chinese Saifun (green bean noodles), Japanese Saifun (potato, yam noodles), rice lasagna noodles, quinoa, soba (buckwheat noodles), quinoa and amaranth pasta products (macaroni) can be purchased in health food stores and health food sections in many grocery stores

Oils:

- Extra-virgin expeller pressed olive oil
- Safflower expeller pressed oil
- Sunflower expeller pressed oil
- Coconut oil
- Flax oil (use only for salad dressings or adding to smoothies)
- (ALL OILS except olive oil and coconut oil must be stored in the refrigerator)
- Earth Balance Natural Buttery Spread® is a low-allergy potential butter/oil substitute found at health food stores, that can be used *after* the Elimination Test Diet when all allergies have been determined.

* 📣 Note

Learning Factors School Aid soft gel capsules should be taken in the recommended amounts every day (Chapter 5) . **Learning Factors School Aid** spoonable liquid can be added to smoothies, to food or salad dressings (1 teaspoon equals 4 capsules).

Herbs & Spices:

- Basil, bay leaves, black pepper, cayenne, cinnamon (ground and sticks), chives, cloves, cumin seed, curry powder, dill, Chinese Five-Spice powder, Herbes de Provence (a rosemary, marjoram, thyme, savory, basil, sage, lavender combination), marjoram, mint, nutmeg oregano, paprika, rosemary, sage, sea salt, tarragon, thyme, turmeric

Condiments:

- Tamari sauce (organic and wheat-free) used very sparingly after completing the Elimination Test Diet
- Dijon mustard, sweet mustard
- Vinegars: apple cider vinegar, rice wine
- See recipes for Allergy-Redux Mayonnaise and Ketchup

Ready-made seasonings:

- Spike® All Purpose All Natural Seasoning (contains a small amount of nutritional yeast. OK in very small amounts)
- Mrs. Dash® Garlic and Herb Seasoning (salt and preservative free)
- Thai spice seasoning, Chinese Five Spice Seasoning
- Gomasio (roasted sesame seeds). Garlic and herb gomasio and seaweed gomasio are available under the Eden Organic® brand
- Nutritional yeast – a food supplement rich in B-vitamin complex. Red Star® nutritional yeast has a particularly cheesy flavour for sauces, soups, and popcorn topping
- Organic vegetable, beef, chicken bouillion cubes or broth mixes

Cans & Jars:

- Avoid canned food as much as possible
- Organic tomatoes (crushed, whole), organic tomato paste, organic tomato sauce, olives, artichoke hearts, salsa (Eden Organic® and Muir Glen® provide a variety of organic tomato products)

Dried Fruits :

- Raisins, apricots, apples, bananas, dates, figs, sun-dried tomatoes (Purchase sulfite-free whenever possible)
- Dried cranberries
- Dried, unsweetened, unsulfited coconut

Nuts & Seeds:

- Almonds, brazil nuts, cashews, hazelnuts, pecans, pine nuts, pistachios, pumpkin seeds, walnuts, sesame seeds, sunflower seeds
- Try to buy nuts and seeds in their most natural forms (unroasted, no added oil, sugar, or salt)

The Elimination Test Diet Refrigerator

Juices:

- Organic juices such as apple juice or apple cider, cranberry juice, pineapple juice, papaya juice, cherry juice, grape juice, lemon juice.

Milks:

- Rice (made from fermented rice) can directly replace cow's milk in most recipes. Use on cereals

- Almond milk and other nut milks - available at health food stores

Vegetables:

- ALL vegetables, preferably organic and pesticide-free.
- Fresh organic garlic
- Fresh organic ginger root

Fruits and Nut Butter Spreads:

- ALL fruits, EXCEPT ORANGES while on the Elimination Test Diet.
- Almond butter, cashew butter, hazelnut butter, EXCEPT PEANUT BUTTER while on the Elimination Test Diet

part II:
tips for preparing food and planning menus

"Human beings do not eat nutrients, they eat food."

Mary Catherine Bateson, cultural anthropologist

as you prepare food for the Elimination Test Diet and healthier eating in general, it is quite likely that you will find yourself and your family members spending more time in the kitchen. You will need to make certain foods in advance and plan your menus carefully. The recipes and tips in this book are not only designed to help you do this as efficiently and nutritiously as possible, but to ensure that you are eating delicious and delightful food which you enjoy!

For the Elimination Test Diet, many initial items must be prepared "from scratch" in order to ensure that you are eating only the ingredients allowed while on the diet. To this end, we have also provided low-allergy potential recipes for common condiments such as ketchup, mayonnaise, sauces, and salad dressings. In addition, you will find recipes for baking powder which are free of aluminum and corn starch.

Also, all the recipe ingredients are presented in the traditional imperial measurement system. For those who prefer to measure in metric, equivalents for both liquid and dry ingredients are presented in a table for your convenience at the start of this section.

Metric Equivalents

liquid	liquid	dry
1/4 teaspoon .... 1 ml	1 fl oz .... 30 ml	1/4 cup .... 50 ml
1/2 teaspoon .... 2 ml	2 fl oz .... 60 ml	1/2 cup .... 125 ml
1 teaspoon .... 5 ml	3 fl oz .... 100 ml	1 cup .... 250 ml
1 tablespoon ...... 15 ml	1 quart .... 1 Litre	2 cups .... 500 ml

Oven Temperatures

fahrenheit	celsius
250° - 275° .... 120° - 140°
300° - 325° .... 150° - 160°
350° - 375° .... 180° - 190°
400° - 425° .... 200° - 220°
450° - 475° .... 230° - 240°
500° - 525° .... 260° - 270°

cooking

About Grains

A variety of whole grains appear in many of the dishes in this book. Despite the North American love affair with bread, very few breads are truly multi-grain. Also, simply eating grains has become neglected in our daily diet, even though these seed-bearing fruits of grasses have been cultivated for thousands of years. Grains are nutritious and easy to cook, combine marvelously with all the food groups, and a multitude of ingredients and seasonings, making them a versatile part of weekly meal planning. In North America, our favourite and most cultivated grain has always been wheat, which is also considered "the staff of life" in cultures worldwide. However, more than 80 percent of the wheat consumed by North Americans is overly refined, resulting in the loss of its bran, its germ, and most of its precious nutrients.

Because wheat is abundant in all our breads, pastas, and most food products, we eat wheat more than any other grain. More than 35 million North Americans currently suffer from intolerances to wheat, probably because they eat wheat with almost every meal from the time of infancy. The Elimination Test Diet requires that you exclude wheat and experiment with a variety of other grains which also offer new earthy, nutty tastes, and rich nutrition. Whenever possible, try to eat organically grown grains to lower your exposure to environmental contaminants.

Cooking Grains

There is no great mystery to cooking grains. For the most part, you prepare grains as you would rice. Wash the grains carefully before placing them in boiling water, add a pinch of salt, cover with a secure lid and cook on low until all the water is absorbed. When cooking more than one cup of grains, it's best to use a wide, heavy pot to ensure the lightness and fluffiness of the grains.

You can greatly enhance the flavour of the grain by using chicken or well-seasoned vegetable broth. With breakfast grains, such as oatmeal or kasha, you can add fruit juices or rice milk as part of the liquid portion. Allow for at least 1/2 cup cooked grain per person for a serving at breakfast, lunch or supper. The following table suggests average cooking times for the grains suggested in this book. Some cooked grains need to stand and remain covered for several minutes before serving. Standing times are noted where necessary.

Grain	Liquid : Grain (Ratio in cups)	Cooking Time	Standing Time
Amaranth	2:1	25 minutes	5 mins
Barley	3:1	1 hour	5 mins
Buckwheat (kasha)	1.5:1	20 min	10 mins
Quinoa	2:1	20 min	
Millet	3:1	20 min	
Rice			
Brown, Basmati	2:1	50 min	
Wild	2:1	2 hours	10 mins

About Beans

Beans belong to the legume family, (which includes split peas, lentils, and peanuts), and have been a crucial part of the human diet for at least 4,000 years. They have a humble reputation in North America as a "poor man's food". Yet, they are one of our richest food sources, a nutrient power pack of protein, vitamins, minerals, zinc, iron, calcium, potassium, magnesium, and the B-complex vitamins. They are also a source of complex carbohydrates, high in dietary fiber, and naturally low in sodium. Recently, beans have become increasingly more popular as we eat more varied ethnically inspired cuisine and discover the limitless combinations of beans, vegetables, and grains to the delight of our palate and the good of our health.

Cooking Beans

Cooking meals with beans does require some pre-planning and preparation. Once you get used to making up a weekly meal planner, this kind of thinking ahead is already organized for you. Dry, not canned beans, are recommended in the recipes in this book. However, at times, you may need to use canned beans for convenience purposes. In such cases, ensure that you drain them thoroughly and rinse them with fresh water to remove as much sodium as possible.

Dry beans always need to be carefully washed, and any pebbles, dirt, sand, or cracked beans need to be removed. Beans need to be soaked over night in three to four times the volume of water in a large pot which will allow for their doubling or tripling in size. This process softens the beans and allows their gas-producing sugars to be released into the water. After the soaking is complete, drain the beans carefully

Quick tip

If you forget to soak your beans overnight, you can soak them for at least four hours which will cut down on their cooking time, or you can cook them for two minutes and allow them to sit for 1 to 2 hours. Then drain and cook as long as needed. Also, salt should not be added to the cooking water, because it prevents the beans from properly softening.

and cook them in a big pot covered with at least 2 inches of cold, fresh water. On high heat, bring them to a boil and then carefully skim off any foam on the surface. Reduce heat to low, and simmer, stirring occasionally until beans are soft and creamy – never mushy.

Dry Bean	Cups of Water	Cooking Time (Approx.)
Adzuki	3	1 hour 15 min
Black beans	4	1 1/2 hours
Black-eyed peas	3	1 hour
Broad	3	2 hours 20 min
Chickpeas (garbanzos)	4	3 hours
Great Northern	3 1/2	2 hours 15 min
Kidney	3	2 hours
Lentils* (green)	3	45 min
(red)	3	30 min
Mung beans*	3	1 hour 10 min
Navy	3	1 1/2 hours
Pinto	3	2 hours
Split peas*	3	1 1/2 hours

Note* : Lentils, split peas, and mung beans do NOT require pre-soaking.

- One cup dried beans makes about 2 1/2 - 3 cups cooked beans.
- One cup canned beans can be substituted for one cup cooked dry beans.

Best Herbs for Beans

Beans, herbs and spices are a winning combination for better taste and better digestion. Certain herbs, known as carminative herbs, help to absorb intestinal gas and decrease the flatulence often experienced after eating beans. You may want to add selections of the following herbs to your bean dishes:

- Anise, caraway, cardamom, cinnamon, coriander, dill, fennel, ginger, and thyme.

About Vegetables and Fruits

Vegetables and fruits are storehouses of vitamins, minerals, antioxidants, and dietary fiber. They also help quench our thirst and act as natural laxatives. In today's seasonless grocery stores we have more access than ever to a diverse collection of vegetables and fruits from all over the world and all year long. Despite the availability of this wide choice of vegetables and fruits, the resounding plea to "Eat your veggies!" appears to be falling on deaf ears as less and less fresh produce makes it on to our plates. Current studies of our North American eating habits reveal that we continue to eat more processed food and more fat than ever before. Children manage to eat only one-quarter of the daily recommended serving of vegetables per day, with French fries making up one quarter of that serving.

In order to encourage eating more vegetables and fruits in our families, we need to serve them at every meal and every snack. Children can be encouraged to clean and peel vegetables and fruits, and make simple dips for pre-supper snacking. You can also sneak grated or puréed vegetables into soups, stews, casseroles, and pasta sauces!

Buying, Storing and Preparing Vegetables and Fruits

Try to buy organic produce in season from reliable health food stores and local farmers' markets, and preferably produce that has been ripened on the plant. Strawberries on the grocery shelf in December and produce transported long distances will have lost a great deal of their original nutrients. How and where fruits and vegetables are grown, whether they were treated with pesticides, fumigants, and fertilizers, how they are stored, when they were picked, and how many miles they have traveled, all greatly affect the nutrients you will eventually consume.

As we cannot always buy certain kinds of fresh produce, frozen produce is the next best choice followed by canned produce. Frozen produce is best steamed to retain maximum flavour and nutrients. Most canned vegetables are overcooked and heavily salted, whereas canned fruits often come soaked in sugary syrup. Carefully drain and wash canned produce before serving to spare your family the extra sodium and sugar.

All fresh produce should be refrigerated in vegetable crispers to maintain freshness and humidity. Frozen produce should be consumed within a couple of months to maintain its taste and nutrient content.

Wash all fruits and vegetables carefully before storing and eating. Scrub the produce lightly with a vegetable brush. You may also use special fruit and veggie 'soaps' now available for removing pesticide build-up on non-organically grown produce.

There are many ways to cook vegetables – steaming, stir-frying, sautéing, boiling, stewing, braising, broiling, glazing, and deep-frying. Cooking vegetables as quickly as possible in a covered pot with a little sea salt preserves their nutrients, whereas cooking them uncovered preserves their colour! For many of the recipes in this book, we recommend steaming. In general, steaming vegetables in a collapsible stainless-steel steamer basket in a large pot preserves most of their colour, nutrients and taste, and helps them to arrive tender-crisp onto

Food IQ Information

Eating fresh produce has declined in North America. Eating fresh apples is down 75%, fresh cabbage down 65%, fresh potatoes down 74%, and fresh melons down 50%. Eating processed fruits has increased 913%, processed vegetables are up 306% and processed fats and oils are up 139%.

Simontacchi, 2000.

your plate. Pressure cookers are also great for saving time and nutrients. Cabbage, onions, garlic, parsnips and turnips are best cooked until they are soft and sweet.

Raw vegetables and fruits are best cut up just before serving. However, preparing veggies and fruit the night before for the next day's lunches is more convenient and ensures that those valuable foods travel with us and are eaten! One serving of a vegetable is equal to one cup.

Cooking and Salad Oils

We recommend cold-pressed, organic oils for cooking, baking, and for salad dressings, sauces, dips, marinades, and spreads whenever possible. The table below indicates the best uses for the suggested oils.

OIL	FLAVOUR	BEST USES
Safflower	nutty-corny	dressings, sautéing, baking, frying
Sunflower	bland	sautéing, baking
Olive	fruity	dressings, light sautéing
Coconut	sweet-nutty	light sautéing
Sesame	nutty	sautéing, dressings
Flaxseed*	nutty-buttery	dressings, dips, spreads
Hazelnut	rich-nutty	dressings, sautéing
Walnut	nutty	dressings, low-heat sauces, sautéing, baking
Almond	sweet-nutty	sautéing, frying, baking

* Do not heat flaxseed oil

Baking for the Elimination Test Diet

Baking with flours other than wheat, and baking without eggs and sugar may seem daunting at first, however, there are a variety of healthy alternatives that will work with a little practice and patience. The following charts will help you as you experiment with the bread, breakfast, and dessert recipes in the next section of this book.

Baking without Eggs

When we bake with eggs, we use them as *binders,* (to prevent crumbling), as *leaveners* (to assist in rising), and as thickeners.

Substitutes for one to two eggs

As a leavener:

- For each egg omitted use 2-3 tsp powdered egg replacer added to the dry ingredients, and 3 1/2 Tbsp water or other liquid added to the wet ingredients.

As a binder and or thickener:

- Combine 1/3 cup water and 3-4 tsp flax seeds. Bring to boil on high heat for 5-7 minutes until a slightly thickened gel begins to form.
- Strain the flax seed out of the liquid and use the gel in the recipes. Substitutes for 1 egg.
- Use 2 tablespoons of fruit purée (such as bananas and apricot mashed together) in baking cakes, sweet breads and cookies)
- Use 2 tablespoons of puréed vegetables in sauces, soups, and other savory dishes.

Low-Allergy Potential Baking Powder

As most commercially made baking powders contain wheat, corn, aluminum, and other additives, you may need to purchase a baking powder at a health food store or custom-make your own.

Recipes for Allergy-Redux Baking Powders

Ingredients

2 Tbsp	baking soda
4 Tbsp	arrowroot powder or tapioca powder
4 Tbsp	cream of tartar

Directions

- Put the above ingredients in a flour sifter and sift them into a bowl. Sift until they are thoroughly mixed.

- Store the baking powder in a tightly closed glass jar in a cool place and use up within 3 months.

- **Note:** Add 5 Tbsp of guar gum (available at health food stores) to the above combination, you will produce an excellent binder in egg-free recipes. However, you must use 1 1/2 times the amount called for in the recipe which uses commercial baking powder.

Ingredients

5 Tbsp	sodium bicarbonate
8 Tbsp	arrowroot powder, potato flour or tapioca flour
7 Tbsp	calcium phosphate (monobasic)

Directions

- Put the above ingredients in a flour sifter and sift them into a bowl. Sift until they are thoroughly mixed.

- Store the baking powder in a tightly closed glass jar in a cool place and use up within 3 months.

- **Note:** Add 5 Tbsp of guar gum (available at health food stores) to the above combination, you will produce an excellent binder in egg-free recipes. However, you must use 1 1/2 times the amount called for in the recipe which uses commercial baking powder.

Baking with Wheat Alternatives

Consult this table when you need to create a wheat-free version of one of your favourite recipes. You will note that some flours are marked with a (B). These flours require a binder such as arrowroot (or an egg replacer), otherwise the baked product will be too crumbly. The flours listed below can usually be purchased at health food stores. If not, you can also make your own flours by grinding the grains in your blender. All flours should be stored in the refrigerator or freezer if not used regularly.

1 cup of Wheat Flour is equivalent to any of the following:

1 cup	Amaranth
1/2 cup	(as a thickener) Arrowroot flour
1/2 cup	Barley flour (B)
3/4 to 1 cup	Buckwheat flour
3/4 cup	Chick pea (garbanzo)
1 cup	(as a thickener) Corn meal or flour
1/2 cup + 1/2 cup	rye, potato or rice flour
1 cup	Millet (B)
1 1/2 cups	Oat flour (B)
1 1/2 cups	Oats (ground, rolled)
3/4 cup	Potato flour
1 cup	Quinoa
1 1/2 cups	Rice (B)
1 1/2 cups	Rye
1 cup	Spelt
1/2 cup	(for sauces) Tapioca
1 cup	(for baking) Tapioca

All of the above flours are suitable for the Elimination Test Diet.

Different Flour Combinations equivalent to 1 cup of wheat flour:

- 1/3 cup potato flour and 1/2 cup rye flour (suitable for Elimination Test Diet)
- 5/8 cup rice flour and 1/3 cup rye flour (suitable for Elimination Test Diet)

Quick tip (when substituting for wheat flour)

- Add 1/2 tsp baking powder for each cup of substitute flour to ensure better rising.
- To improve texture, refrigerate the dough for 1/2 an hour before baking.

Alternative Sweeteners

How to adapt recipes that contain sugar

Once you begin reading labels more carefully, you will discover that sugar is often among the top three ingredients in most prepared foods, and is of course a starring ingredient in most baked goods. While on the Elimination Test Diet, we encourage you to greatly cut down on your sugar intake, including diluting your fruit juices with reverse osmosis or distilled water.

However, for adults and children who are used to regularly consuming a lot of sugar in their diet, such a change may be too drastic for both the taste buds and the body. The table below suggests alternative sweeteners to white and brown sugar. Once you become accustomed to cooking and baking without sugar, you will realize that you can satisfy a craving for something sweet, while also eating food which is healthier and more nourishing for your brain. The Dessert recipes in this cookbook will convince you of that!

Some alternative sweeteners are sweeter tasting than others. You can decide which ones suit your needs, taste, and food budget.

Quick tip

- When using any wet concentrated sweetener such as honey in place of sugar, reduce liquid content in the recipe by 1/4 cup. If no liquid is called for in the recipe, add 3 - 5 Tablespoons of flour for each 3/4 cup of concentrated sweetener. Add about 1/4 tsp of baking soda to the recipe and lower the oven temperature by 25 degrees to prevent over-browning. Follow these same suggestions for maple syrup.

- Heat thick syrups before working with them by setting their jars in hot water for 5 - 10 minutes. Be sure to first oil the measuring utensils used with the thick syrups.

- Some malted sweeteners (brown rice or barley malt) may liquefy the consistency of the mixture. This is more likely if eggs are in the recipe, which is not a problem on the Elimination Test Diet. To prevent the mixture from becoming too liquid, you can boil the malt syrup 2-3 minutes before using it. Let it cool slightly first before adding it to the recipe.

This list is divided into Dry Sweeteners (dry, granulated sugars) and Liquid Sweeteners (liquid sugars).

- The sweetest alternatives are presented first, followed by the less sweet options.
- You can interchange most of these sweeteners. For example, 1 cup of honey can be replaced with 1/2 cup of brown rice syrup and 1/2 cup of date purée.
- Replace 1 cup of white or brown sugar with any one of the following sweetener alternatives below:

Dry Sweeteners:

1 cup Sucanat® (dried organic cane juice)

1 cup Fruitsource® (granulated rice syrup and grape juice concentrate)

1 cup ground date sugar

1/3 to 1/2 tsp Stevia* white extract powder

1 1/2 to 2 Tbsp Stevia Plus™ powder

18 to 24 Stevia Plus™ packets

Liquid Sweeteners:

1 cup maple syrup

1 cup sorghum

1 cup concentrated fruit sweetener

1 cup barley malt

1 cup brown rice syrup

1 cup puréed dates

1 cup apple butter

1 cup frozen fruit juice concentrate

(NO **orange juice** during Elimination Test Diet)

1 cup fruit juice (NO orange juice)

1 tsp *Stevia Clear Liquid™

2 tsp *Stevia whole leaf dark liquid concentrate = 1 cup brown sugar

1 cup agave syrup (natural fructose from cactus)

Food IQ Information

*Stevia is the sweetest herb! A teaspoon of dried stevia leaves is sweeter than a cup of sugar without the calories, and it does not raise blood-sugar levels or promote tooth decay. It is stable in both hot and acidic conditions, making it perfect for baking and cooking, and for sweetening fruit vinegars. However, Stevia does not caramelize like sugar, so it cannot be used in making meringues. Stevia extracts are available and are free of the somewhat grassy taste found in ground Stevia leaf.

Help with Meal Planning

"Never eat anything at one sitting that you can't lift."
Miss Piggy

What you plan to eat will determine what you have to buy for the week. Planning requires considering the needs of the Elimination Test Diet and choosing what you think you or your family members are most likely to eat. A quick scan of the Foods Allowed and the Recipes in the last section of this book should reassure you that there is more than plenty to eat despite the restrictions of the diet!

Once you have made those decisions and have all the ingredients at your fingertips, it is much easier to stay the course of the Elimination Test Diet because you will always be prepared with the exact foods you need. Preparing some foods over the weekend helps reduce your daily time commitment to food preparation. Planning for a weekly menu also helps ensure that you are eating a variety of foods and balanced meals throughout the week.

Portions

A basic rule for determining food portions is simply to divide your plate into four sections. One section should contain a complex carbohydrate such as a whole grain, one a protein such as meat or beans and pulses, and the other two should include fruit and/or vegetables.

While this is not always possible or necessary for every meal, an overview of your daily and weekly menu will reveal the balance or imbalance in your choices. Remember that a snack can always make up for a missing portion at a meal. It is important, however, that breakfast include protein and complex carbohydrates in order to beat the mid-morning sugar or coffee cravings.

Refer to the table on the following page which includes recipes* from this book and a sample Weekly Menu Plan. A blank weekly planner for your menus and your shopping list is provided for you at the end of the book to photocopy and personalize for you and your family's tastes and requirements.

In order to make your shopping and your food preparation somewhat easier and less complicated, you will find that many of the recipes in this book (like those with an * in the menu plan below) contain the same, readily available ingredients. Buying one ingredient that does the job best makes it easier. Occasionally you will need to find an exotic spice for some Asian or Indian inspired dishes, if you choose to prepare them.

A Balanced Meal

W E E K L Y   M E N U   P L A N

Meals	Mon	Tues	Wed	Thurs	Fri	Sat	Sun
Breakfast	Cooked oatmeal with apples and Rice milk	Rice & Raisin Breakfast pudding* (use rice from supper	Banana-Nut Smoothie*	Fresh Fruit Wake-Up*, Rice Crackers with Cashew butter	Quick and easy muesli*, sliced bananas with nut butter	Oatmeal with almonds and Rice milk	Quick Buckwheat-Oat Pancakes Strawberries*
Mid-Morning Snack	Sesame Bar*	Celery sticks filled with almond butter	Mixed nuts	Zucchini-Carrot muffin*	Earth Balls*		
Lunch	Left-over Lentil Tomato Vegetable soup*	Left-over chicken, Sunflower salad*	Cool Colour Crunch Salad* with ham or meat of choice	Left-over beef on rye bread, allergy-free Mayo*, lettuce & tomatoes	Left-over Sweet Chicken stir-fry in a rice wrap	Salmon salad* on rice crackers, Cherry tomatoes, Apple	Surprise Pasta salad* with sliced turkey meat
After-School Snack	Very Berry Smoothie*	Earth Balls*, Fruit	Fruit Pick-Ups*, Sesame Bar*	Raw veggies with cold ratatouille as dip	Flatbread with Hummus*	Blueberry Blast Smoothie*	Oatmeal cookies*
Supper	Herbed Chicken, Basmati Rice, Dilled Green beans*	Halibut, Hot Veggie salad, Small red potatoes w/ herb butter*	Beef stew meat topped w/Ratatouille*	Sweet Chicken stir-fry*	Macaroni and "Cheese"*& Broccoli	Pork Chops w/home-made apple sauce, baked fries, Green peas	Lentil Tomato vegetable soup* with Flat bread*

See pages 256-257 for a blank weekly menu plan for photocopying

146

Make your Favourite Recipes Allergy-Redux

What about my family's traditional favourite recipes?
As there may be only one child or adult on the Elimination Test Diet (ETD) in your household, you will still want and need to prepare some of your family's favourite recipes. The Ingredient Substitution List suggests some workable alternatives for converting your traditional recipes to allergy-redux versions. The Recipe Conversion Samples illustrate how this can be done.

Modifying recipes often for the ETD requires some experimentation. Don't give up! When you get it right, record the exact variations you made in your notebook for guaranteed success the next time.

INGREDIENT SUBSTITUTION LIST	
Ingredient	Substitution
Dairy	
Milk	Rice milk, nut milks (almond, cashew, brazil)
Cheese	"Parmesan" topping: Red Star Nutritional Yeast, "Mock Cheese" Recipe: (see page 220) Use as "Cheese" spread, "Cheese" filler for lasagna, Soymage (casein-free)
Butter	Clarified Butter (Ghee, see page 218), Oils: Sunflower and saflower expeller cold pressed oils for cooking and baking, olive oil and coconut oil for cooking and sautéing, Spreads: combine 50% coconut oil and 50% flax oil, NO MARGARINE
Eggs	Egg whites, egg yolks. As a binder use: 2-3 tsp powdered egg replacer per egg, or liquid lecithin with 2 tsp guar gum as a leavener use: 1 tsp aluminum free baking powder per egg.
Mayonnaise	Eggless oil mayonnaise, tofu based mayonnaise, egg free, soy-free mayonnaise (page 215)
Sugar White and brown sugar	Stevia (1 tsp Stevia = 1 cup sugar), Sucanat, honey, maple syrup, rice syrup, fruit concentrate syrup, unsulfured molasses, agave nectar, amazake (rice culture sweetener), Xylitol, Sorbitol, small amounts of powdered fructose. Organic apple cider, grape juice, fruit concentrates, NO NUTRI-SWEET OR ASPARTAME
Orange Juice Whole, juice, concentrate, flavouring	Lemon, lime, pineapple, carrot, papaya, cranberry, raspberry, apple, cherry
Vinegar	Lemon juice
Peanuts Whole nuts, butter, oil	Cashews, almonds, pistachios, brazil nuts, walnuts, pine nuts, hazel nuts. Cashew butter, almond butter
Chocolate	Carob
Wheat Flour	Brown rice, white rice, rye, amaranth, quinoa, teff, spelt, barley, oat, chickpea flour
Wheat Noodles	Arrowroot noodles, buckwheat noodles, rice noodles
Wheat Crackers	Rice crackers, cassava crackers
Whole Grains	Barley, oats, rye, amaranth, quinoa, teff, buckwheat

oatmeal cookies

Traditional Ingredients

1/2 cup	butter
1/2 tsp	baking soda
1 cup	sugar
1/2 tsp	salt
1	egg
2 1/2 cups	oatmeal
1/3 cup	milk
1/2 cup	raisins
1 1/2 cups	flour
1/2 cup	chopped nuts
1 tsp	cinnamon

Allergy Redux Version
(Substitute Ingredients)

6 Tbsp	safflower oil
6 Tbsp	rice or milk
1 tsp	cinnamon
1/2 cup	maple syrup or other liquid sweetener
1/2	baking soda
1 egg =	1 Tbsp psyllium seed husks and 2 Tbsp water (egg replacer)*
1/2 tsp	sea salt
1/2 cup	rice flour
2 1/2 cups	oatmeal
1/2 cup	oat bran
1/2 cup	raisins
1/2 cup	oat flour
1/2 cup	chopped nuts

Directions

· In a medium mixing bowl, mix the safflower oil, rice milk, egg replacer, and maple syrup and beat well, ensuring all ingredients are well blended.

· Gradually mix in the dry ingredients until everything is well combined. Add the raisins and the nuts.

· Use a teaspoon to drop batter on an ungreased cookie sheet.

· In a 350° oven, bake the cookies about 8 minutes, or more if you want them to be crispier.

*You can also use commercial egg replacer. (Brand name: EnerG)

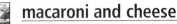

macaroni and cheese

Traditional Ingredients

1/2 lb	durum wheat macaroni
2 Tbsp	margarine
2 Tbsp	flour
2 cup	milk
1 tsp	prepared yellow mustard
1 cup	grated cheddar cheese
1 tsp	salt
1 tsp	pepper

Allergy Redux Version
(Substitute Ingredients)

(Makes 6 one cup servings)

1/2 lb	rice or quinoa or spelt macaroni
2 Tbsp	clarified butter or safflower oil
2 Tbsp	barley flour
2 cups	plain rice milk
1 tsp	prepared yellow mustard
1 cup	Mock Cheese Sauce (no soy, no dairy) See page 220
1 tsp	sea salt
	Safflower oil

Directions

· Boil 4 quarts of cold water in a large pot. Add macaroni to the water and cook according to the directions on the package. While the macaroni is cooking, prepare the sauce.

· To make the sauce, heat the clarified butter or oil in a saucepan, and stir in the flour with a whisk. Beat quickly until smooth.

· Pour in the rice milk and cook, stirring with the whisk until the mixture thickens and is not lumpy.

· Remove the saucepan from the heat, and add in salt, pepper, and mustard.

· Stir the mock cheese into the saucepan and keep it warm.

· Drain the cooked macaroni and place in a casserole dish oiled with the safflower oil. Pour the "cheese" sauce over the macaroni and bake in a 400° oven for 20 minutes.

· Serve with mixed veggies on the side.

apple cinnamon flan

Traditional Ingredients

1 3/4 cup all-purpose flour

1/2 tsp baking powder

1 large egg

6 Tbsp sugar

5/8 cup soft margarine

4 large cooking apples, pared and thinly sliced

1 tsp cinnamon

6 Tbsp brown sugar. Toss together and set aside

Grease a glass pie plate. Bake about 1 1/2 hours.

Allergy Redux Version
(Substitute Ingredients)

2 cups brown rice flour

2 Tbsp tapioca

1/2 tsp baking powder (aluminum free)

1 Tbsp ground flax

3 Tbsp water or rice milk

3 Tbsp Sucanat

1/4 cup sunflower oil (organic, expeller-pressed)

4 large cooking apples, pared and thinly sliced

1 tsp cinnamon

6 Tbsp Sucanat

Directions

·   Grease a glass pie plate with oil and flour pan.

·   Mix the oil and sucanat. Beat in the flax and water. Sift together the flour and baking powder and fold into mixture. Dough should be spreadable. Top up with rice milk if necessary. Cover with sliced apple mixture.

·   Bake about 45 mins to 1 hour. Serve warm or cold as a dessert.

Do I need any special utensils or tools for these recipes?

None of the recipes in this book require special cooking utensils or tools, although *a good blender* (preferably with a glass bowl) is a must for making soups, batters, salad dressings, sauces, purées, shakes, smoothies, and for grinding grains into flours.

Food processors are also very handy for vegetables, bread dough, and chopping nuts. They are not necessary, but are great time-savers.

A stainless steel collapsible vegetable steamer that you can pop in a sauce pan is also handy for obtaining maximum nutrients from your vegetables, and *a wok style pan* is great for stir-frying.

For those who may be wheat and gluten intolerant, *a bread machine* is a good investment for making low-allergy potential breads, as they can be difficult to find and also expensive if purchased regularly.

What Not to Use For Your Food Preparation

Avoid using cookware coated with Teflon-like coatings. When heated to above 500° F, polymer fumes are released, and 15 toxic gases and chemicals, including two carcinogens.

Use stainless steel, cast iron, glass, porcelain or enamel cookware instead.

Refrain from using a microwave as much as possible. Microwave cooking and reheating significantly decrease the nutritional value of your food.* Microwaving in plastic containers releases plasticizers into the food and negatively affects its taste. Fatty foods such as meat and cheese are most easily contaminated. *Never* microwave human milk as it will lose its infection-fighting factors. If you must microwave food, use glass containers.

*A recent 2003 study revealed that "nuked" broccoli loses up to 97 percent of some of its nutrients, especially health-promoting flavonoids.

conscious eating
"to eat is human;
to digest is divine"

Charles Townsend Copeland

as you prepare your food for the Elimination Test Diet and try some of the recipes in this book, you will become more conscious of both the nutritional and psychological benefits of eating wholesome, high-energy, low-sugar, low-allergy potential food. While WHAT you eat is important for maximum brain and body performance, HOW you eat is equally important for 'divine digestion'.

In a society where food is becoming increasingly valued for how cheaply we can buy it, how quickly we can prepare it and how fast we can eat it, the art of actually enjoying and digesting the food we eat is being sacrificed. To best digest food we need to pay attention to what we are eating and how we are eating it. In other words, we need to be fully conscious when eating and digesting. Eating while in the car, at the fast-food court, standing at the sink, walking down the shopping mall, eating while working, not taking time to chew food carefully and "washing it down" with water or pop, are all habits conducive to stressful digestion and poor absorption of nutrients. Unfortunately, many of our public schools contribute to instilling these kinds of habits in our children who are rarely given more than 15 minutes to eat their lunches every day at school, and are provided with brain zapping snack choices in school vending machines.

To become a more conscious eater and to ensure better digestion, you will need to examine the way you and your children eat, and to consider the following suggestions:

Take your time when eating, savour every bite, enjoy family or other good company whenever possible during meals.

- Try to avoid being constantly distracted while eating. Focus on the moment, the joy of your meal and the fellowship of friends and family.
- Avoid eating on the run or eating in a big rush. If you are pressed for time, make a nutritious smoothie!
- Sit down when eating and sit up straight.
- Take small bites, chew food well and avoid gulping in air while talking and chewing.
- Avoid gulping liquids during meals. Ideally, try to drink several minutes before each meal.
- Eat only when hungry and stop before you are completely full.

- Try to eat no later than three hours before retiring to bed.

For your children:

- Find out how much time your child has for eating lunch at school. Advocate for more time if necessary.
- Promote better food choices for school "fun lunches" and provide alternatives to soda pop in the school vending machines.
- Above all, prepare and eat food that delights your eye and your palate and makes you feel good – as long as it is healthy!

part III:
the recipes

" The preparation of good food is merely another expression of art, one of the joys of civilized living."

Dione Lucas

he recipes in this book have been carefully chosen for their nutritive value, their healthful, mostly low-allergy potential ingredients, their relative ease of preparation and their great taste! All recipe creations are the results of combined efforts from many people who care about food. These recipes come from the kitchens of health conscious cooking experts, including nutritionists, medical and naturopathic physicians, healthy-food oriented restauranteurs, and many mothers. Several recipes are also inspired by other cultures and cuisines, introducing novel taste sensations and hopefully some new family favourites!

For our purposes here, these recipes have been adapted to suit the strict requirements of the Elimination Test Diet. With time and practice, you will likely change these recipes to suit your own special needs and tastes. Preparing brain and body-healthy food will soon become second nature as you learn to combine different ingredients and create your own meals from your well-stocked pantry and refrigerator. You will also want to seek out new ideas from other cookbooks and health-savvy friends. Some of the larger health food stores often offer cooking classes for people concerned with allergies or offer free, in-house potential recipes you can take back to your kitchen. The recipes in this book are all dairy, wheat, egg, soy, corn, citrus, and baker's yeast free.

In his book, *The Physiology of Taste*, Anthelme Brillat-Savarin states that "The discovery of a new dish does more for human happiness than the discovery of a new star." We hope that these new dishes will inspire you to discover both the happiness and health of nutritious, conscious eating!

Recipes

brain booster
breakfasts

Current nutritional studies confirm that Mom was right (again!). Breakfast is the most important meal of the day. A good breakfast improves concentration, memory, mood, and energy levels. Children who skip breakfast or gobble down sugar-laced cereal, donuts or the like, are tired in school, apathetic, irritable, can't focus, and are often hyperactive. They may have behaviour problems and struggle with problem solving and learning.

In our morning haste to get out the door on time, breakfast is often eaten "on the run" — a breakfast which does little to keep our brain and body well stoked for the day ahead. Many breakfasts consist of refined carbohydrates which result in a "fast burn," leaving us shaky and sleepy by mid-morning, frantically searching for a coffee or a sugar-fix.

A Brain-Booster breakfast requires a *balance* of protein and carbohydrates, and the right fat and fiber to ensure optimal brain function. Planning and preparing ahead are the keys to ensuring that healthy breakfasts appear on the table on time, and are eaten sitting down. The recipes and suggestions in this section are designed to help you achieve that goal.

You can make low-allergy potential, nutrient -packed muffins, granolas, breakfast bars, and multi-grain, high-fiber pancakes and waffles on the weekends which can be frozen and then reheated to get your day off to a great start. We recommend using left-overs for breakfast

Food IQ Information

The diets of most children in Western societies are far from perfect. In the 1999 report of the Federal Interagency Forum on Child and Family Statistics, a large U.S. Government research agency, it was reported that most children and adolescents have insufficient diets. In fact, dietary problems were found to increase significantly as children grew older. According to this research, 76 percent of children ages 2 to 5, 88 percent of children ages 6 to 12, and 94 percent of children ages 13 to 18 had a diet that was poor or needed improvement. This same report stated that 1 in 5 adolescents between 13 and 18 years of age had diets that were judged as "poor", that is, they were seriously malnourished. Breakfast, even though it is the most important meal of the day is, unfortunately, the most likely to be inadequate.

in creative ways, chopping up fruit the night before, and making delicious and nutritious smoothies with a whir of the blender! You can also check out our list of "Quick Picks for Breakfast."

Quick Picks

Cold cereals
Puffed rice and puffed millet can be poured into a bowl and served with rice milk and chopped fruit. Packaged cold cereals made from quinoa, millet, amaranth and other multi-grain (or ancient grain) combinations which contain no wheat, added sugar or additives can be found at health food stores and many grocery stores in the natural foods section.

Homemade granola or muesli can be served up in a jiffy. (See Recipes – pages 169,167)

Hot cereals
Many hot quick-cooking cereals can be prepared in less than 10 minutes on the stove top such as cream of rice, oatmeal, oat bran, kasha (buckwheat cereal), or any hot cereals which do not contain wheat or corn.

Ants on a log
Slice bananas lengthwise, spread with cashew or almond nut butter and add raisins for 'ants on a log'!

Pre-chopped and chilled fruit prepared the night before
Apples, apricots, bananas, blackberries, blueberries, cantaloupe and other melons, cherries, cranberries, grapes, dates, figs, kiwis, mangoes, nectarines, papayas, peaches, pineapple, plums, prunes, raisins, raspberries, strawberries, watermelon are all acceptable on the Elimination Test Diet. They add vitamins, antioxidants, and fiber to breakfast fare.

Unsalted nuts and raw seeds
Almonds, Brazil nuts, cashews, hazelnuts,

macadamia nuts, pecans, pistachios, sesame seeds, sunflower seeds, pine nuts, and walnuts, can be tossed into hot or cold cereals for crunch, taste, and added protein, calcium, zinc, B vitamins and magnesium.

Left-overs

Rice cakes and rye crackers can be served with nut butters, or slices of meat or chicken left-over from supper. Whole left-over cooked potatoes can be sliced up or chopped into chunks and lightly sautéed.

Re-heat

Pre-frozen, pre-made high-fiber waffles, pancakes, muffins and breakfast breads can be reheated in the toaster or toaster oven and served with prepared chopped fruit or accompanied by a Learning Factors Smoothie! (See Super Smart Smoothie Recipes on page 173)

Juices

Apple, cranberry, carrot, papaya, prune, grape, pear, pineapple WITHOUT added corn syrup, sugar, glucose, or colourings.

banana zinger muffins

Ingredients

(Makes 1 dozen muffins)

2	ripe, medium bananas, mashed
1/3 cup	pure, maple syrup
2/3 cup	pineapple juice*
1/3 cup	safflower oil
2 tsp	fresh ginger root, finely grated
	or
1 tsp	powdered ginger
1 tsp	lemon zest, finely grated
1 cup	rice flour
1 cup	spelt flour
1 tsp	aluminum free baking powder
1 tsp	baking soda
1/2 tsp	sea salt
1 cup	coarsely chopped pecans, toasted

Directions

· Preheat the oven to 350°F. Oil a 12-cup muffin pan with safflower oil and dust with flour.

· Combine the banana, maple syrup, pineapple juice, oil, ginger and lemon zest in a medium-sized bowl.

· In a large bowl, whisk the flour, baking powder, baking soda, and salt together until well combined.

· Add the wet ingredients from the medium bowl to the mixture in the large bowl and combine, being careful not to overmix the batter. Stir in the pecans.

· Spoon the batter into the prepared muffin pan so that each cup is about 3/4 full.

· Bake until a toothpick inserted into the center of a muffin comes out clean, about 20 to 25 minutes

· Allow muffins to cool before taking them out of the pan.

* use freshly squeezed orange juice after ETD, if tolerated

quick blender buckwheat-oat pancake waffles

Ingredients

(Makes 8-10 pancakes
or waffles)

1 cup	rolled oats, uncooked
1/2 cup	buckwheat flour
1/4 tsp	salt
1 1/2 tsp	aluminum free baking powder
1 1/4 cups	rice milk (or water)
1 Tbsp	safflower oil
1 Tbsp	honey
1/2 cup	dried cranberries (optional)

Directions

· Place oats in blender. Grind into a coarse flour.

· Add remaining ingredients and blend well.

· Let batter sit 2 - 4 minutes to thicken.

· Blend again for 30 seconds.

· Pour onto hot, greased griddle or into oiled waffle iron.

· For pancakes, cook until bubbles form on the top, and then flip over to brown.

· Serve with fruit of choice.

zucchini-carrot bread or muffins

Ingredients

(Makes 1 loaf or 12 muffins)

1/2 cup	cooked millet*
1/2 cup	finely grated zucchini
1/2 cup	finely grated carrot, well-packed
1/2 cup	crushed pineapple, drained
3/4 cup	honey, maple syrup, or fruit concentrate
1/4 cup	safflower, cold-pressed oil
1/2 cup	apple, pear or peach juice
1-2 tsp	vanilla extract
2 cups	oat flour
2 tsp	guar gum (available at health food store)
3-4 tsp	aluminum-free baking powder
1/4 tsp	sea salt

Optional:

1/2 cup	raisins or chopped nuts

Directions

· Preheat the oven to 350ºF for bread, 375-400ºF for muffins. Lightly oil a large loaf pan or muffin pan. Lightly flour the pan and shake out excess.

· Mix all the wet ingredients together thoroughly and gently.

· In a separate bowl, sift together the flour, guar gum, baking powder, and sea salt.

· Combine the wet and dry ingredients thoroughly. The batter should be stiff. Fold in raisins or nuts. Scoop batter immediately into pan or muffin pan and spread smooth.

· For bread, bake 55 - 60 minutes until bread is lightly browned and a toothpick comes out clean.

· For muffins, bake for 20 - 40 minutes.

· Cool 15 minutes or more before removing from pan.

*To cook millet; wash thoroughly. Use 3 1/2 - 4 cups water to 1 cup millet. Bring water to a boil and add millet. Simmer gently for 30 minutes. Drain well before adding to recipe.

quick and easy muesli

Ingredients

(Makes 4 generous servings)

4 cups	rolled oats
1 cup	slivered almonds or chopped walnuts
1/4 cup	sesame seeds, ground
1/4 cup	flax seeds, ground
1/2 cup	sunflower seeds, ground
1-2 tsp	cinnamon
1/4 tsp	sea salt

Directions

· Mix all ingredients together and refrigerate until ready to eat. All nuts can be ground in a blender 1/4 cup at a time at high speed, or ground in a food processor with the metal blade.

· To eat, soak a half a cup of the mixture in boiled water for 15 - 20 minutes

· Serve with rice milk or nut milk, and honey.

fresh fruit breakfast compote

Ingredients

(Makes 8 servings)

4	ripe bananas, sliced in chunks
2 cups	fresh pineapple chunks (or canned and drained)
2 cups	seedless grapes, halved
2 cups	cherries or strawberries
1/2 cup	pineapple juice

(Optional: 2 tsp honey)

Directions

· Toss and mix well.
Chill before serving to blend the flavours

nutty maple granola

Ingredients

(Makes 6-8 servings)

5 cups	organic rolled oats
1/2 cup	oat bran
1/4 cup	raw pumpkin seeds
1/2 cup	unsalted sunflower seeds
1/2 cup	sliced almonds
1/2 cup	chopped pecans
1/4 cup	chopped walnuts
1/2 cup	sunflower oil
1/2 cup	pure maple syrup
2 tsp	ground cinnamon
3 Tbsp	barley malt syrup

Directions

- Preheat the oven to 350°F. Lightly oil a large baking pan, or use two pans

- Combine the oats, oat bran, all nuts and seeds in a large bowl. Thoroughly mix in the cinnamon.

- Mix the sunflower oil, maple syrup, and barley malt in a separate bowl.

- Pour the maple mixture into the large bowl and stir well to completely coat the dry ingredients.

- Carefully and evenly spread the granola on the baking pan.

- Bake for 15 to 20 minutes. Stir every 5 minutes to guarantee even baking, until the granola begins to smell and turns a golden colour. Remove the pan from the oven immediately to allow it to cool. Store the granola in a large glass jar or ceramic container.

rice potato pancakes

Ingredients

1/2 cup	rice flour
1/3 cup	potato flour
1/4 tsp	salt
1/2 tsp	baking powder
1/3-1/2 cup rice milk	

Beat together:

1 1/2 tsp	safflower oil
1 1/2 tsp	rice milk
1 tsp	baking powder

Directions

· Sift rice and potato flours, and salt and 1/2 tsp baking powder together.

· Beat in 1/3 to 1/2 cup rice milk.

· Beat in mixture of oil, rice milk and 1 tsp baking powder

· Cook in a hot pan oiled with safflower oil and use 1/4 cup batter for each pancake.

· Carefully turn over once to ensure even browning on each side.

· Add extra rice milk if necessary

raisin-rice breakfast pudding

Ingredients

(Makes 4 servings)

3 cups	cooked brown rice (Basmati is best)
1/2 cup	raisins
1/4 cup	pure maple syrup
1/2 cup	coarsely chopped raw almonds or other nuts, toasted (optional)
1 tsp	ground cinnamon
1/2 tsp	ground nutmeg
1 cup	vanilla rice beverage to be added when serving.

This dish is a great way to use up last night's left-over rice

Directions

· Put all ingredients into a medium saucepan and stir together.

· Bring to a boil over medium-high heat, then reduce the heat to low and simmer, stirring often to avoid scorching, until thickened (about 5-8 minutes).

· Serve immediately in individual bowls and add rice milk to taste.

super
smart smoothies

Smoothies are an easy, refreshing, nutritious smart start to the day, (especially for any late risers who might be rushing off to school). You need a blender and a freezer stocked with various different smoothie ingredients to make them exactly when you want them! Smoothies are also great as after-school, after-work snacks, and summer time cooling alternatives to soft drinks.

Preparing the ideal and most brain-nutritive smoothie at breakfast or for any time of day is super easy when you use Natural Factor's Learning Factors Smoothie Mix available in both natural and wild berry flavours. Learning Factors Smoothies are an ideal way to ensure that everyone will get his or her daily nutrient boost.

Reluctant breakfast eaters and late-riser teenagers will all enjoy and benefit from this "shake to go." Made from low-allergy potential, highly-digestible vegetable-derived protein, Learning Factors Smoothie mix contains the full range of brain-critical minerals and vitamins including: calcium, magnesium, iron, zinc, selenium, chromium, manganese, potassium, iodine, phosphate, copper, and high quantities of B, C, E, A, and D vitamins. It also incorporates Grape Seed extract to protect the brain from oxidative stress and Milk Thistle extract to protect the liver from toxic stress. The added fiber from guar gum and cellulose fiber help detoxify the liver and offer powerful prebiotic properties.

Nick: The Groggy Teenager Wakes Up!

Nick was the typical late-riser teenage boy who never had time for breakfast, and was always chasing the school bus. He dozed through his morning math classes to the detriment of his grades, and was often plagued with headaches throughout the day. At my suggestion, his mother began making him a Learning Factor's Smoothie every morning, a convenient and brain-power packed "fast food" he could drink on the bus en route to school. Recently, Nick went out of his way to tell me how drinking the breakfast smoothie was keeping him alert for his morning classes, that he had aced his last math test, and he had no more headaches!

Combined with the fruit, nuts, and juice of your choice, the Learning Factor Smoothie is a sure winner for starting everyone's day off right!

Basic Ingredients

Any fruits, melons, or berries (frozen or fresh) can be used. Strawberries are probably the best fruit to start with because they taste fantastic in a smoothie and are very easy to freeze. Bananas also taste great, and can add a nice smooth texture to a smoothie. Peel the bananas when they are well ripened, and freeze them in zip lock freezer bags.

Try to find organically grown fruit whenever possible. Using frozen fruit eliminates having to add ice cubes for those who like a cold smoothie. Any fresh berries picked during the summer season can be frozen on cookie sheets in your freezer and then transferred to freezer bags making them easy to defrost when needed for smoothie making. Over-ripe fruit is also excellent for tossing in the blender. Get into the habit of looking for slightly overripe fruit on sale, buying as much as you can afford and freezing the fruit for future use. Organic apple cider juice works well with most all fruit and berry combinations. Other juices or fruit-based herbal teas can also be added.

· To make any smoothie, you can generally count on using 1 to 1 1/2 cups of liquid with 1/2 cup of fruit, adding supplements (Learning Factors Smoothie Mix) and sweeteners if desired. Blend all ingredients until the mixture is smooth. Add more liquid for a thinner consistency.

· To give body and added nutrition to the smoothie, the following ingredients work well: plain yogurt (with bacterial cultures), silken tofu, flax oil, bananas, frozen rice drink and/or pineapple juice (prepared in ice cube trays). Flax oil is also a welcome addition.

(**NOTE:** Yogurt and tofu are NOT permitted while on the Elimination Test Diet. Instead, use bananas which make an excellent thickener in place of yogurt and tofu).

· To add sweetness, 1/2 tsp Stevia extract powder or 3 - 4 drops Stevia liquid extract can be added to the entire mixture, or honey or maple syrup to taste.

· To add brain nutrition, add 2 scoops of Learning Factors Wildberry Flavour Smoothie Mix or Learning Factors Natural Unflavoured Smoothie Mix!

banana-nut smoothie

Ingredients

(Makes 1 serving)

1	medium banana (frozen and cut into chunks)
1 cup	cold water
8	Brazil nuts
2 scoops	Learning Factors Smoothie Natural Unflavoured Mix
1 1/2 tsp	carob powder (optional)
	Maple syrup to taste

Directions

· Put Brazil nuts and water into blender.

· Grind the nuts on low speed first, then on high, until blended to a smooth paste. Scrape sides of blender with a spatula if needed.

· Add the frozen banana, Learning Factors Smoothie Natural Unflavoured Mix, carob powder (optional), and maple syrup to taste. Blend on high speed until smooth and creamy. Add water for your desired consistency.

very-berry boost

Ingredients

(Makes 1 serving)

(Fresh berries are ideal, however, an equal portion of a frozen berry mix will work too)

1/4 cup	raspberries
1/4 cup	strawberries
1/4 cup	blueberries
1/2 cup	rice or nut milk
1/2 cup	organic apple cider
2 scoops	Learning Factors Smoothie Mix

Directions

· Blend all ingredients at high speed until smooth.

blueberry blast

Ingredients

(Makes 1 serving)

1 cup	blueberries
1/2	frozen banana, broken into chunks
1 cup	organic apple cider
2 scoops	Learning Factors Smoothie Mix

Directions

· Blend all ingredients at high speed until smooth.

tropical treat

Ingredients

(Makes 1 serving)

1 1/2 cups unsweetened pineapple juice

1/2   medium frozen banana, cut into chunks

1/4 cup Mandarin orange sections

2 scoops Learning Factors Smoothie Mix

Honey to taste or 3-4 drops of Stevia liquid extract or 1-2 Tbsp Stevia Plus powder

Directions

·   Blend all ingredients at high speed until smooth. Add ice cubes for a cooling tropical drink.

fresh fruit wake-up

Ingredients

(Makes 2-3 servings)

1 cup	fresh strawberries
1	banana, cut into chunks
2	pears, peeled and sliced
4 Tbsp	lemon juice
1/2 cup	grapefruit juice
1/2 cup	apple cider juice
1 cup	unsweetened grape juice
4 scoops	Learning Factors Smoothie Mix
	Honey to taste or 3-4 drops of Stevia liquid extract or 1-2 Tbsp Stevia Plus powder

Directions

· Blend all ingredients together on high.

wonderberry sorbet

Ingredients

(Makes 6 - 8 servings)

1 cup — puréed frozen mixed berries, (strawberries, raspberries, blueberries, blackberries)

2 cups — organic apple cider juice

4 scoops — Learning Factors Wild Berry Flavour Smoothie Mix

8 drops — Stevia liquid extract or honey to taste

Directions

· Blend the organic apple juice and the Learning Factors Wild Berry Flavour Smoothie Mix in the blender on high speed, until the mix is mostly dissolved.

· Add the puréed frozen fruit, and the desired sweetener, and blend on high speed until creamy in texture.

· Pour mixture into an ice cream maker and process for 30 - 45 minutes until it develops a sorbet-like consistency. Serve immediately or place in freezer for a couple of hours for a firmer texture.

· If you do not have an ice cream maker, place the mixture in a covered container and freeze until it becomes sorbet!

luscious
lunches

Lunch time is a welcome mid-day break, however, many of us do not look forward to preparing and packing lunches! In North America, lunch often travels as a sandwich. The Elimination Test Diet presents additional challenges to this tradition, as wheat flour and yeast cannot be eaten during the dieting period.

What can I possibly pack for Elimination Test Diet Lunches?

Whether you are preparing lunch for adults or children on the Elimination Test Diet, it helps to think "outside the sandwich." Think of lunch as a great time to present left-overs in new and creative ways, including last night's soup, and rolling up yesterday's extra rice or potato salad in a wrap. There are so many different ways of packaging your usual sandwich fillings!

Start with **rice paper wrappers**, which solve the problem of finding or making low-allergy potential breads. 8 - 12 inch round rice wrappers can be used for both cold and hot fillings. They are ideal for wrapping up left-overs or for the salads and rice dishes suggested here.

Refer to the "How to Make a Wrap" Diagram on page 189 for further guidance.

Veggie wrappers such as romaine or leaf lettuce, cabbage or chard leaves can be also used to roll up fillings. Celery sticks can be filled with nut butters, and green peppers, avocado halves, scooped out tomato, zucchini or cucumber halves can also be stuffed. (See Suggestions in Desserts & Treats) All these little packages can be eaten out of hand with little mess or fuss.

Lentil papadams are flat spicy, lentil flour breads, and can carry pizza style toppings. Papadums are usually available in the "foreign food" section of your grocery store.

Chapatis are a flatbread made from chick pea or garbanzo flour and can also be used as sandwich bread substitutes on the Elimination Test Diet (See recipe on page 194)

Rice crackers are also an option.

Many low-allergy potential breads are now available at health food stores and bakeries. If you want to bake your own, some suitable Elimination Test Diet bread recipes you can make by hand or in a bread machine can be found in "Our Daily Bread" section.

Once you have completed the Elimination Test Diet, and have determined what you can eat, other "wrapper" and sandwich bread substitutes may include corn tortillas, taco shells, pita pockets, crèpes, different ethnic flatbreads, and your favourite grain based breads, pumpernickels, rye breads, manna breads (sprouted, unleavened bread), spelt and flax breads, hot dog buns, and rolls.

PLANNING is essential before preparing or packing lunches and cuts down on your stress factor. We recommend you spend at least one hour a week planning the weekly menu and writing up your grocery list for breakfast, lunch, snacks, and supper. During the Elimination Test Diet all sandwich condiments will need to be made in advance. (See "Salad Dressings, Sauces, Spreads, Dips & Mock Cheese" section)

Thinking of lunch "outside the sandwich," will require you to add a food thermos and vegetable and salad containers to your lunch bag or box.

Home-made soups are usually welcome in colder weather days. We suggest a lunch container with a stackable three component tray so that veggies, fruits, and snacks can be conveniently separated without using additional plastic wrapping.

In this section, you will find some sample lunch combinations suitable for the Elimination Test Diet, cross-referenced with recipes and suggestions found throughout the recipe section of this book. You can use these combinations to make up a weekly menu, and then design your own weekly menu according to your personal tastes and the time you have for food preparation.

What to drink and how much?

Water is always preferable to juices at lunch time. We recommend drinking water that has been treated through the process of reverse osmosis. Distilled water has had all the minerals removed, so it is less desirable. Reverse osmosis (RO) water is readily available at most larger grocery stores and health food stores where you can bring in your own jugs for refills. You can chill your water bottle beforehand and add a swig of lemon or lime juice for more zing!

Most people do not drink enough water and are therefore often dehydrated. Unfortunately, water is often replaced with coffee, pop and fruit juice which cannot replace water's job in our bodies. In fact caffeinated drinks reduce the water available to us.

On the average, we need to drink between 8 and 10 glasses of water a day. Ideally, you should drink water relative to how much you weigh, the climate you live in, and your activity level. Normally, a 110 pound woman needs 8 cups a day, whereas a 200 pound man would need at least 12 cups or more.

On the following pages are some sample lunches you can try.

Lunch Sample #1:

Salmon Salad Sandwich (see Recipe p. 203)
using low-allergy potential bread

1 cup of strawberries (or seasonal fruit)

Veggie chips ("Terra Chips" brand, Snyder's Veggie
Crisps, or Mister Krispers)

Sesame Bar for mid-morning snack
(see Recipe p. 242)

Lunch Sample #2

Brown rice cakes with nut butter
(cashew or almond)

Carrot and Jicama sticks
(sprinkled with salt, cayenne, or lemon juice)

Nut and/or raw seed mix

Apple

Lunch Sample #3

Macaroni and "Cheese" (see Recipe p. 150)

Celery sticks filled with nut butter

Lentil Tomato-Vegetable Soup (if you're inspired!)
(see Recipe p. 234)

Earth Balls (see Recipe p. 243)

Lunch sample #4

Rice wraps with chicken and rice
(see Chicken Wrap Recipe p. 188)

Coleslaw (See coleslaw combos p. 205)

Blueberries

Lunch sample #5

Chapatis bread with 1/4 cup hummus
(see Chapatis Recipe, p. 194, see hummus recipe
p. 221)

Green beans
(see Recipe for Dilled Green Beans, p. 207)

Pear

curried chickpea and potato wrap

Ingredients

(Makes 12 wraps)

12	8 inch rice paper wrappers (or 8 inch corn flour tortillas; when not on the ETD)
1 tsp	safflower oil
1/2 cup	finely chopped red onion
2 cloves	garlic, minced
1	small jalapeno pepper, seeded and minced (optional)
1 Tbsp	curry powder
1 tsp	ground cumin
1/4	sea salt
2	medium potatoes, peeled, and diced small
1/4 cup	water
15oz can	chickpeas, rinsed and drained
2/3 cup	fresh or frozen peas
3 1/2 cups	shredded red cabbage

Directions

· Preheat oven to 250°.

· Heat oil in large skillet over medium heat. Add onion, garlic and jalapeno and cook. Stir frequently until onion is soft, about 2 minutes.

· Add curry powder, cumin and salt and cook, stirring, 2 minutes more.

· Add potatoes and water; cover and cook until veggies are tender about 10 minutes. Add chickpeas and peas. Cover and cook 5 minutes.

· To assemble: Spoon 1 - 2 tablespoons filling into each wrap and top with shredded cabbage. Roll wraps around filling and cabbage. Serve warm if possible, or cold in a lunch box.

chicken wrap

Ingredients

(Makes 4 servings)

4	rice paper wrappers
2 Tbsp	tamari (organic and wheat-free)
1 Tbsp	honey
1	small clove garlic, minced
2	thin slices ginger root, finely shredded
1 lb	chicken meat (or left-over cooked chicken meat)
2	green onions, sliced on the diagonal
	Chinese Five Spice Seasoning or Thai Spice Seasoning, to taste
2 Tbsp	coconut oil
1 1/2 cups shredded lettuce	

Directions

· Prepare rice paper wrappers as indicated on p. 189

· In a small bowl, mix tamari, honey, garlic, and ginger root

· Heat coconut oil in large skillet over medium heat. Add the above mixture and bring to a simmer, stirring constantly.

· Add chicken and stir to coat thoroughly. Cook over high heat for about 4 minutes, and add your choice of seasoning to taste. Toss in the scallions and cook until soft.

· Left-over brown rice or coconut rice may be added to the chicken for a heartier wrap. Top with shredded lettuce.

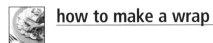 # how to make a wrap

To prepare rice wraps, you simply hold them under gently running cool water for 10 seconds on each side and then carefully lay them on a clean towel to soften. Try layering two together for extra strength and place a layer of plastic wrap on top. More can be added two at a time with a layer of plastic wrap between each pair. Wraps will be soft and ready for use in 2-3 minutes.

1 Place fillings around the center of the rice wrap

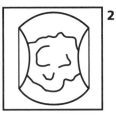

2 Bring in both sides of the rice wrap and begin to roll from the bottom up

3 Continue to roll up towards the top of the rice wrap

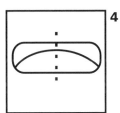

4 Cut in half and enjoy the great taste of rice wraps

our daily
bread

"When the bread rises in the oven, the heart of the baker rises with it."

Frederica Bremer

For most of us, bread is a staple and a comfort food in our daily fare. During the Elimination Test Diet, you are required to give up eating wheat and yeast risen bread. As rice is the most low-allergy potential grain, we have recommended using rice paper wraps to keep life simple for the time you are following the diet. Non-wheat and yeast free breads can be purchased at specialty bakeries, health food stores, and some grocery stores. However, for those of you who would like to make your own bread, we have included some recipes which meet the strict requirements of the Elimination Test Diet. While making alternative grain bread without the usual help from yeast and eggs can be a challenge at first, you can be successful with some extra patience and experimentation.

We refer you back to "Tips for Preparing Food and Planning Menus" in Section Two, Part 1 for helpful information on baking without eggs and sugar, and using alternative grains.

barley sandwich bread

Ingredients

(Makes 1 loaf)

3 cups	barley flour, (divided into 2 1/2 cups and 1/2 cup)
2 tsp	guar gum (available at health food store)
1 tsp	sea salt
2 cups	water
3/8 cup	safflower oil
1 1/2 tsp	baking soda
1/2 tsp	unbuffered Vitamin C crystals

Wheat-free & Yeast-free Bread

Directions

· Using an electric mixer, combine 2 1/2 cups of the flour, guar gum, and the salt in bowl. Add the water and the safflower oil and beat the dough for 3 minutes on medium speed.

· Combine the remaining 1/2 cup of flour with the baking soda and Vitamin C crystals, and stir them immediately into the dough mixture in the bowl.

· Beat the mixture on medium speed for 30 seconds.

· Place dough in an oiled and floured 8" by 4" loaf pan and bake at 350° for 55 - 65 minutes, or until a toothpick inserted in the center of the loaf comes out dry.

· Remove the bread from the pan immediately.

flatbread

Ingredients

(Makes 8 pieces)

1/2 cup	barley, buckwheat, or amaranth flour
1/2 cup	brown rice, oat or tapioca flour
2 tsp	arrowroot powder
1/2 cup	water
2 tsp	safflower oil
1/3-2/3 cups	extra flour for kneading

Directions

· Preheat oven to 400°

· Mix the two types of flours together thoroughly with arrowroot powder. Keep mixture in separate bowl.

· Mix oil and water together and add this to the flour mixture. Work it together with a fork and then with your hands.

· Knead a bit and roll the dough into a ball. Divide into 8 parts.

· Roll each part into a ball and pat it flat.

· Using a rolling pin and extra flour, roll each bread between two sheets of waxed paper. Turn over frequently while rolling. Use enough flour so dough does not stick.

· Lightly oil a frying pan and heat it until it is fairly hot.

· Put one bread (flattened to about 1/8" thick) in the frying pan. Heat 15 - 20 seconds on each side.

· Then put the bread immediately into the pre-heated 400° oven for 3 minutes on the first side and then turn it over for 1 - 2 minutes on the second side.

· The bread should puff up a bit like traditional pita bread.

· Re-oil the frying pan before heating each bread.

· Cool the finished breads before storing.

chick pea chapatis

Ingredients

(Makes 8-10 chapatis)

1 cup	chick pea flour (garbanzo bean flour)
1/3 cup	water
2 Tbsp	arrowroot powder
1 Tbsp	safflower oil

Optional:

1/4 tsp	sea salt

Directions

- Mix all ingredients well. Roll into 1" balls and pat flat. With a rolling pin, roll out pastry-like rounds.

- Heat a lightly oiled frying pan until very hot. Reduce heat to medium-high and heat each round for 1-2 minutes on each side, until warmed and slightly browned.

- Serve hot or store in the refrigerator.

- Serve with rice and curried foods, and use as a bread substitute for sandwiches.

quick and simple banana bread

Ingredients

(Makes 16, 1 inch slices)

1/4 cup	rice milk (for Elimination Test Diet)
6 Tbsp	safflower oil
6 Tbsp	pure maple syrup or Sucanat
2 1/4 cups	mashed ripe bananas (about 5 medium bananas)
1 1/2 cups	rice flour
1/2 cup	tapioca flour
2 Tbsp	roasted grain beverage powder *
1 tsp	baking soda
1 tsp	aluminum free baking powder
1/2 tsp	sea salt
1 cup	walnuts

Directions

· Preheat the over the 350°F. Lightly oil an 8"x 8" cake pan and dust with flour.

· Put the rice milk, oil, maple syrup, and bananas in a blender and blend until smooth.

· In a large bowl, whisk the flour, beverage powder, baking powder, baking soda, and salt until well combined.

· Add the banana mixture and combine, using as few strokes as possible. Do not overmix.

· Fold in the walnuts.

· Scrape into the cake pan and smooth the top. Bake for about 30 - 35 minutes, or until a toothpick inserted into the centre of the bread comes out clean.

· This banana bread is a favourite with most children and is great at breakfast, and can be packed to travel for lunch.

*roasted grain beverage powder is made from roasted grains such as barley, rye or wheat, often flavoured with malt, beet root, or chicory. When dissolved, they produce a coffee like flavour without the caffeine. They are available in health food stores under the brands Inka™ and Krakus.™ Krakus™ is wheat-free.

Adapted from John Robbin's
"May All Be Fed: Diet for a New World," 1992.

bread machine rice bread

Ingredients:

(Makes 1 loaf: 16 servings)

1 1/3 cup	brown rice flour or white rice flour
1/3 cup	tapioca flour
1/3 cup	potato flour
2 3/4 tsp	guar gum (available at health food stores)
2 3/4 tsp	aluminum free baking powder
3/4	salt
1 Tbsp + 1 tsp	safflower oil
1/2 cup	egg replacer*
1 1/3 cup	water

Directions

Mixing:

- First, put the flour(s), baking powder, salt, and guar gum in the bread machine. Press START and mix for 1/2 to 1 minute.

  Do not add all the ingredients at once.

- Add the safflower oil and mix for 1 minute.

- Add the egg replacer and the water.

- At the end of the mixing time, use a rubber spatula to ensure that the dough is evenly distributed and covers the bottom of the pan.

Cycle: Quick bread or cake

* When not on the Elimination Test Diet, 2 large eggs may be used instead of the egg replacer.

From Nicolette M. Dumke's
"Easy Bread Making for Special Diets", 1995.

lunch box bread

Ingredients

(Makes 8 hearty servings)

1 cup	light rye flour*
1 cup	white rice flour
2 tsp	aluminum free baking powder
1 Tbsp	powdered ginger
1 tsp	cinnamon
3 Tbsp	safflower oil
1/2 cup	light unsulfured molasses
1/2 cup	water
3 Tbsp	crystallized ginger, finely chopped (optional)

Directions

Do not add all the ingredients at once.

· Preheat the oven to 350°. Grease and flour one 9" x 9" pan.

· Sift together the flours, baking powder, powdered ginger and cinnamon.

· In a large bowl, beat the flour mixture and safflower oil together.

· Gradually beat the 1/2 cup of molasses, water and crystallized ginger (if using).

· Scrape the batter into the prepared pan. Bake until a toothpick inserted into the center comes out clean, 35 - 40 minutes. Allow the gingerbread to cool 10 minutes in the pan on a rack, before serving. Let the bread cool right side up on the rack.

This is a favourite for lunch boxes!

* When not on the Elimination Test Diet, spelt flour may be substituted.

salads,
fruits & veggies

"Salad refreshes without weakening and comforts without irritating, and it makes us younger."

Brillat-Savarin, French gastronome, 1825

It is not surprising that the word salad comes from the Latin *salus* which means "to bring health." The French say "Salut!" when they drink to your health.

The Greeks considered salad to be a food of the gods. Truly healthful salads consist of a combination of fresh, organically grown, pesticide-free greens, and /or vegetables, fruits, nuts and seeds. A salad can be a complete meal or a side dish. Salads can also include a variety of vegetables, grains, beans and pasta. Dressed in additive-free nutritive oils and herbs, salads should radiate health.

The typical North American version of salad is a combination of iceberg lettuce, faded, often flavourless tomatoes, and a few gratings of carrots and random bits of bell pepper, drenched in a high cholesterol, high fat, and additive packed dressing, is more likely to bring you indigestion than health and to consume almost half your necessary calorie intake for the day.

Healthy salads need not be boring or complicated. Simple tossed green salads composed of crisp romaine lettuce, butter lettuce, oak leaf lettuce, a mix of baby greens, mung bean sprouts, served individually or combined, can be mixed with a simple dressing such as olive oil and lemon juice and are easy to prepare for the Elimination Test

salads, fruits & veggies

Diet or anytime. Unsalted nuts and seeds can be tossed in the salad for added protein, minerals and extra crunch. See the "Salad Dressings, Sauces, Spreads, Dips, and Mock Cheese" for ways to add more to your salads.

The salad recipes to follow use a variety of ingredients that can be easily modified to your taste and time! Many of these salads are a complete meal and can be easily rolled and wrapped for your lunchbox. For children who will not eat salad, keep raw veggies on hand, especially served with a tasty dip such as hummus (See Recipe, p. 221). Remember to keep the fridge stocked with a variety of vegetables and fruits for snacking, and involve the children in making the dips.

Quick tip

Tired of the same old greens for tossed green salads? Try some of these green suggestions: Arugula, artichokes, asparagus, avocados, bib lettuce, beet greens, Belgian endive, Chinese cabbage, cucumber, curly endive, dandelion greens, escarole, kale, mustard greens, oakleaf lettuce, radicchio, romaine lettuce, Savoy cabbage, sorrel, and watercress.

mediterranean quinoa salad

Ingredients

(Makes 4 servings)

2 cups	quinoa (uncooked)
4 cups	boiling water
1	red or yellow bell pepper
1/2	small purple onion
8-10	sun dried tomatoes
1/4 cup	pine nuts
1/2 cup	chopped parsley
2 Tbsp	freshly squeezed lemon juice
1/3 cup	olive oil
2	garlic cloves
1 tsp	Dijon mustard
1/2 tsp	sea salt

Directions

- Rinse quinoa well. Bring four cups of water to a boil in a medium saucepan. Add quinoa and lower to simmer. Cook for 15 minutes. Set aside in a large bowl and cool completely.

- Toast pine nuts on a cookie sheet at 300° F until fragrant and lightly browned.

- Chop bell pepper, onion, and sun dried tomatoes into small pieces. Finely chop parsley.

- In a small bowl combine lemon juice, olive oil, garlic, mustard and salt.

- Toss dressing, veggies and cooled quinoa together. Sprinkle with toasted pine nuts.

- Enjoy as a side dish or as a complete meal.

Contributed by Commonsense Cookery, Victoria, BC

sunflower salad

Ingredients

(Makes 4 servings)

2 cups	coarsely shredded carrots
1 cup	thinly sliced celery
2	firm bananas, sliced
1/2 cup	sunflower seeds
1/4 cup	sunflower or safflower oil
2 Tbsp	unsweetened pineapple juice
1/4 tsp	sea salt
1/4 tsp	pepper
	Romaine lettuce leaves

Directions

· Combine the carrots, celery, banana, and sunflower seeds. Stir the oil, juice, salt, and pepper together. Pour over the salad mixture and toss lightly. Serve on lettuce, or WRAP a serving with a rice wrap!

 **salmon salad**

Ingredients

(Makes 3 cups)

2 cups	drained canned salmon (packed in water)
1/4 cup	diced yellow onion*
1 cup	diced celery
1 cup	egg-free, soy-free mayonnaise (p. 215)
1/2 tsp	sea salt
	Pepper to taste

Directions

· Mix all ingredients together and store in refrigerator.

· Serve over lettuce, in sandwiches or wraps.

*Onion may be omitted if preferred

surprise pasta salad

Ingredients

(Makes 4 servings)

5-6 oz	rice pasta (shells, spirals, or elbows)
1	6-oz can salmon drained
	(or 1 cup chopped cooked chicken, or 1 cup chopped ham)
1/4 cup	chopped onion (or chopped dill weed)
1	stalk celery, chopped
1	dill pickle, chopped (optional)
1 cup	chopped black olives (optional)
1/4 cup	chopped red pepper or pimento (optional)
2-3 Tbsp	homemade mayonnaise* to taste
	*(See Mayonnaise Recipe under *Salad Dressings, Sauces, Spreads, Dips, and Mock Cheese*, p. 215)

Directions

· Cook pasta according to package directions. Drain pasta well and add all ingredients. Toss well.

 **coleslaw combos**

Ingredients

(Makes 6 servings)

4 cups	shredded cabbage (half green, half red if preferred)
2 cups	shredded carrot
	Diced apple and raisins

Dressing

Tart

1/2 cup	homemade mayonnaise (see page 215)
1 tsp	apple cider vinegar (or lemon juice)
1/8 tsp	salt
	Black pepper to taste

Sweet

Use equal amounts of pineapple juice in place of vinegar or lemon juice

Also add your favourite herbs. Dill, celery seed, chopped parsley, chives are some options.

Directions

· Coleslaw combinations are always versatile and can be customized to suit your family's taste buds. These are some basic ingredients to start with. The dressing can be either tart or sweet.

cool colour crunch

Ingredients

(Makes 6 Servings)

2 cups	cooked, fresh grated beets (or canned and drained if necessary)
1 1/2 cups	shredded red cabbage
1/2 cup	shredded green cabbage
2 cups	grated carrots
1	orange (use juice and zest)
1 Tbsp	red wine vinegar (or lemon juice)
1/2 tsp	ground fresh ginger
1/2 tsp	sea salt
1 tsp	sesame oil
	Herbs: chopped parsley, cilantro, or chives
	A handful of raw cashew nuts, or peanuts, blanched, slivered almonds, or roasted sunflower seeds

Directions

· Combine beets, cabbage, carrots, and herbs of choice, and toss well in a large mixing bowl.

· Whisk the orange juice, zest, vinegar (or lemon juice) ginger, salt, and oil in a small bowl.

· Scatter unsalted nuts or seeds of choice over top.

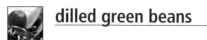

dilled green beans

Ingredients

(Makes 6 to 8 Servings)

2 lbs	fresh green beans, ends trimmed
3 Tbsp	safflower oil
1 Tbsp	tapioca flour
2 Tbsp	horseradish (drained)
1 1/4 cups rice milk	
	Sea salt and black pepper
1/2 cup	fresh dill, finely chopped

Directions

· Cook beans in salted water until tender.

· Heat oil in saucepan. Add flour and horseradish and stir constantly for 1 minute.

· Mix in rice milk.

· Bring to a boil. Reduce heat and simmer for 2 minutes.

· Add the salt and pepper.

· Stir in the dill and pour sauce over top of the beans.

· Serve hot.

hot veggie salad

Ingredients

(Makes 4 - 6 servings)

3 cups	broccoli, chopped
2 cups	cauliflower, chopped
4	carrots, peeled and sliced on the diagonal
1	red pepper, diced
1	leek, finely sliced on the diagonal
	OR
	4 green onions

Lemon Dressing

(Makes 3/4 cup)

1 tsp	water
1/8 tsp	sea salt
1/8 tsp	grated lemon rind
2 tsp	dried mint
2 fl oz	fresh lemon juice
1/2 cup	Gomasio seeds (roasted sesame seeds)
	Freshly ground black pepper to taste

Directions

Dressing

· Make the lemon dressing in advance. Put water, salt and lemon rind in a jar with a tight lid. Let stand for several minutes. Add mint and lemon juice. Put the lid tightly on the jar and shake. Add the olive oil and black pepper. Shake again to blend well.

· Steam the broccoli, cauliflower, leeks and carrots until they are tender. Drain and add the diced red pepper.

· Pour the dressing over the salad while hot. Sprinkle on gomashio seeds.

salad dressings,
sauces, spreads, dips and mock cheese

The food you prepare for the Elimination Test Diet and happily thereafter, need never be bland! This selection of low-allergy potential condiments will ensure that all the food you prepare will be either savoury, tangy, sweet or cheesy, satisfying all the different tastes in your household.

almond miso sauce

Ingredients

(Makes approx. 3/4 of a cup)

4 Tbsp   almond butter

3 Tbsp   miso (any type)

1-2 Tbsp   pure maple syrup

1/4 cup   hot water
           (not boiling)

Directions

·   Combine almond butter, miso and maple syrup to form a thick paste. Slowly add hot water until desired consistency is reached.

·   Use this sauce to dress up lightly steamed veggies, grains or other simple meals.

·   If reheating this sauce be careful not to bring it to a boil as the beneficial micro-organism in miso cannot withstand excessive heat.

herb butter

Ingredients

3-4 Tbsp unsalted clarified butter*

(1 Tbsp per person), softened at room temperature

1/4 tsp finely chopped garlic

1/4 tsp finely chopped shallots or onions

1/2 tsp of any one of the following fresh herbs: dill, chives, tarragon, rosemary, parsley

Salt and pepper to taste

Directions

· Place all the ingredients in a shallow bowl and combine well. A herb butter is not a melted butter and is served in a solid form. Add salt as needed. This butter may be served over fish or vegetables.

* See recipe for clarified butter on page 218

fruit purée

Fall/Winter ingredients

1	pear
1	apple
1	banana
1/2 cup	rice milk

Spring/Summer ingredients

1	peach or 2 apricots
1	plum
1	pear
1	banana
1/2 cup	rice milk

This purée replaces eggs in baked goods which require an egg as a binder.

Directions

- For either combination, put all the ingredients in a blender and blend until smooth and the consistency of a milkshake.

- Four or five pieces of fruit will yield enough purée for two batches of muffins, cake or fruit bars. Will keep for about 5 days in a tightly covered container in the fridge.

egg-free, soy-free mayonnaise

Ingredients

(Makes 1 1/2 to 2 cups)

1 1/2 Tbsp	rice flour
1/2 tsp	salt
1/4 tsp	dry mustard
1/4 cup	cold water
3/4 cup	boiling water
1/2 cup	safflower oil
1/4 cup	apple cider vinegar (or lemon juice)
1/8 tsp	paprika
	Sea salt and pepper to taste

Directions

· Combine the flour, salt, dry mustard, and cold water and stir well. Add the boiling water. Stir constantly over medium heat until the mixture thickens and comes to a boil. Cool until lukewarm. Combine the vinegar and oil and add to the mixture slowly, beating constantly. When well blended, beat in the paprika and salt and pepper. Refrigerate in a covered container.

berry dressing

Ingredients

(Makes 1 1/2 cups)

1 cup	fresh or frozen raspberries or strawberries
1/2 cup	pure water
1/2 cup	sunflower oil
1/2 tsp	sea salt (optional)
1 tsp	paprika
	Add honey to taste or 1/2 tsp Stevia powder if you want a sweeter taste

Directions

· Pour water, oil, seasonings and honey in a bowl and whisk together. Stir in berries and mix well.

· Perfect for a tossed green salad, spring mix and fresh spinach, and poured over cooked, cubed beets.

homemade ketchup

Ingredients

(Makes 1 3/4 cups)

12 oz can	organic tomato paste
1/2 cup	cider vinegar
1/2 cup	water
1/2 tsp	sea salt
1 tsp	oregano
1/8 tsp	cumin
1/8 tsp	nutmeg
1/8 tsp	pepper
1/8 tsp	mustard powder
	Squeeze of garlic from press

This ketchup is free of additives and sugar.

Directions

· Mix all ingredients together. Store in a jar in the refrigerator.

Clarified Butter or Ghee

If you're allergic to dairy, you may miss the wonderful flavour of butter on your toast and in your baking and cooking. Many people can tolerate a clarified version of butter or what is known as ghee in India. Make your own and see if it works for you.

· You will need 1 lb of *unsalted* butter.

· Heat the butter in a heavy-bottomed saucepan over low heat. Be careful the butter doesn't brown. After one hour the butter will have melted and separated. Skim off and discard the whey and milk solids that sit on top of the liquid. Pour the remainder through a strainer so you are left with a golden liquid or ghee. Use it in place of oil. It can be spooned when thick or poured when liquid. You can also add your favourite spices or fresh herbs to create a savoury spread.

· Store the ghee in a covered glass container and refrigerate.

marvelous maple balsamic vinaigrette

Ingredients

(Makes 1 cup)

3	garlic cloves, peeled and minced
1/4 cup	balsamic vinegar
1 Tbsp	fresh lemon juice
1 1/2 tsp	pure maple syrup
1 1/2 tsp	Dijon mustard
1/2 tsp	sea salt
1/4 tsp	cracked pepper
1 Tbsp	Red Star nutritional yeast
3/4 cup	flax seed oil or extra virgin olive oil

Directions

· Combine all ingredients except the oil and then slowly add oil and continue mixing until all ingredients are blended.

mock cheese sauce

Ingredients

(Makes 1 serving)

2 cups	water
1/4 cup	tomatoes
1/4 cup	raw almonds
1/4 tsp	garlic powder
1/2 tsp	onion powder
1/2 Tbsp	sea salt
1/2 Tbsp	fresh lemon juice
2 Tbsp	arrowroot powder
1/4 cup	Red Star nutritional yeast

Directions

· Blend all ingredients in blender until very smooth.

· Pour in 2 quart saucepan and cook on medium heat until thick, whisking continually.

· Use as a cheese sauce for macaroni or vegetables.

mediterranean hummus

Ingredients

(Makes 12 servings)

19 oz	can Chickpeas, (Garbonzo beans) drained
1/4 cup	tahini
1-3	garlic cloves (or to taste)
1/2 tsp	sea salt
1/4 cup	lemon juice (or to taste)

Directions

· Combine all ingredients in a food processor or blender. Blend for 2-3 minutes to a smooth paste. (Add water if thinner texture is desired).

· Pour into a serving bowl and garnish with olive oil and a sprig of parsley, fresh mint or lemon wedges and green onions.

bean dip

Ingredients

(Makes 2 cups)

16 oz	Cooked beans: chick peas, black, white, or kidney beans
2	shallots or 1 onion
1/2 cup	chopped leeks
2 cloves	garlic, minced
1 Tbsp	cashew butter
3 Tbsp	chopped fresh parsley
1 Tbsp	olive oil

Directions

· In a small skillet, heat oil on medium heat. Add leeks, shallots or onions and garlic. Sauté for 5-10 minutes or until leeks are soft.

· While vegetables cook, add remaining ingredients to a food processor. When vegetables are cooked, add to bean mixture.

· Process until all ingredients are well mixed and texture is creamy. Allow to cool before eating.

Adapted from Bastyr University Natural Health Clinic

supper
selections

For supper, select recipes from any section of this book and combine them to suit your family's needs and tastes. Above all, remember to keep supper simple — for example, a salmon steak with herb butter and some lemon broccoli, with rice or potatoes, or a chicken breast served with dilled green beans, brown rice and carrot sticks, meet all the requirements of the ETD and provide balanced nutrition.

Soups, Stews, Stir-Fries & Oven Dishes

Homemade soups and **stews** are time-honoured comfort foods which provide sustenance for the body and soul. They also require spending some time in the kitchen and can involve willing family members (almost all ages!) in their initial preparation. Once all the ingredients have been added to the pot, with some time and a little watching, a magic merger of flavours develops, and the final medley is most welcome. Soups and stews are convenient one-pot nourishment, and can be stored in the fridge for several days or frozen up to four months. Great reheated, they can be your best fast food!

Soups and stews are best cooked in non-reactive, stainless steel pots, some which may be coated with enamel. Slow-cookers or crockpots are also ideal, as you can leave the pot cooking all day and arrive home to the simmering elixir of ready-made delicious and nutritive food.

Stir-fries satisfy our need to prepare and eat great tasting and healthful food in short order. They are also one-dish meals, packed with a variety of ingredients which you can cook up quickly, and have time left over to savor the results! Because stir-fries are so versatile, you can easily create your own originals by using up your left-over veggies, meats, and rice. Stir-fries are best prepared in heavy skillets or stainless steel woks, preferably flat-bottom woks for electric ranges.

TIP: Make great soup stock which you can keep frozen until soup or stew making time.

Save your left-over water from steamed vegetables to make soup stock. Vegetable scraps and peelings and any uncooked left-overs can be cooked on low heat for 30 - 60 minutes to add to the stock. Strain all veggies and reserve the liquid. Toss any leftover cooked vegetables into your blender and puree them for stock.

TIP: Prepare ingredients for stir-fries ahead.

Many of the ingredients for stir-fries can be chopped and measured the day before cooking. Try to slice meats and veggies the same size and thickness to ensure uniform cooking. Make the sauce the night before and remember to marinate the meat if needed. Pre-cook the rice or pasta needed in the recipe or use your left-overs!

The following recipes make nutritious and delicious lunch or supper selections.

you can't beet borscht soup

Ingredients

(Makes 8 servings)

2	medium beets, steamed
1	medium carrot, steamed
2 cups	green cabbage, shredded, steamed
1	medium cucumber
1	medium green bell pepper, coarsely chopped
1 large	yellow onion, finely chopped
2 Tbsp	safflower oil
1	lemon, juiced
1-2 Tbsp	honey
1	ripe avocado, peeled, stone removed and quartered
1/2 cup	fresh dill, chopped
2 Tbsp	tamari (organic and wheat-free)
2	bay leaves
1/8 tsp	black pepper
1 tsp	sea salt
4 cups	vegetable stock or bouillon
	Fresh dill for garnish

Directions

· Steam the beets and carrots until tender. Reserve the vegetable liquid to add to stock to make 4 cups of stock

· Pulse the beets, carrots, cucumber, bell pepper, and lemon until finely chopped (in a food processor or in a blender, adding small quantities at a time).

· Add the avocado, dill, tamari, salt and black pepper. With the machine running, add the stock and process until smooth.

· In a large pot, sauté the onion in the safflower oil until tender, adding the shredded cabbage until tender as well.

· Transfer the rest of the vegetables to the pot and add the stock.

· Stir, cover and simmer on low for 30 - 45 minutes.

· Remove bay leaves, adjust seasonings, and serve hot. Garnish with dill.

· Add dollops of fresh plain yogurt if dairy is tolerated after the ETD.

provençal turkey soup

Ingredients

(Makes 4 - 5 servings)

1 Tbsp	olive oil
2	red, yellow or green bell peppers, cored, deseeded and finely chopped
1	stalk celery, thinly sliced
1	large onion, finely chopped
14 oz can	organic plum tomatoes in juice
3-4	garlic cloves, finely chopped
4 cups	turkey or chicken stock
1/4 tsp	dried thyme
1	bay leaf
2	zucchini, finely chopped
12 oz	cooked turkey, cubed
	Sea salt and pepper
	Fresh basil leaves to garnish

Directions

· Heat olive oil in a large saucepan over medium heat. Add the bell peppers, celery and onion and cook for about 8 minutes until softened and beginning to colour.

· Add the tomatoes and garlic.

· Stir in the stock. Add the thyme and the bay leaf. Season with salt and pepper and bring to a boil. Reduce the heat, cover and simmer for about 25 minutes until the vegetables are tender.

· Add zucchini and turkey. Cook for another 10 - 15 minutes until the zucchini are completely tender.

· Test taste the soup and adjust the seasoning. Ladle into warm bowls and garnish with the bay leaves.

brown rice & and black-eyed pea soup

Ingredients

(Makes 4 - 6 servings)

9 oz	dried black-eyed peas
1 Tbsp	olive oil
1	large onion, finely chopped
2	garlic cloves, crushed
2	carrots, finely chopped
2	celery stalks, finely chopped
1	small red bell pepper, deseeded and finely chopped
3 oz	lean smoked ham or smoked salmon, finely diced
1/2 tsp	fresh thyme leaves,
	or
1/8 tsp	dried thyme
1	bay leaf
5 cups	chicken or vegetable stock
2 1/2 cups	water
1/2 cup	brown rice (Basmati if possible)
	Chopped fresh parsley or chives to garnish

Directions

NOTE: Requires over-night preparation for soaking the peas.

· Prepare the peas: Soak and Pre-cook.

· Select the best peas and cover them with plenty of water in a large bowl or pot. Allow them to soak for at least 6 hours or overnight. Drain the peas. Put them in a saucepan and add enough cold water to cover by 2 inches (5 cm). Bring to a boil and boil for 10 minutes. Drain and rinse well.

· Heat olive oil in large heavy-based saucepan over a medium heat. Add onion and cover and cook for 3 - 4 minutes. Stir frequently until softened.

· Add garlic, carrots, celery and bell pepper. Stir well and cook for an additional 2 minutes.

· Add the drained peas, ham or salmon, bay leaf, stock and water. Bring to a boil, reduce the heat, cover and simmer gently for 1 hour or until peas are tender. Stir occasionally.

· Stir in the rice and season the soup with sea salt and pepper if desired. Continue cooking for 30 minutes or until rice and peas are tender.

· Taste the soup and adjust the seasoning. Serve in warm bowls and garnish with parsley and chives.

sweet chicken stir-fry

Ingredients

(Makes 4 servings)

1 cup	mushrooms, sliced
12 oz	boneless, skinned chicken breast halves
2	medium red, green, orange or red sweet peppers, seeded, cored, cut into strips
2	medium red apples, thinly sliced
2 cups	pre-cooked basmati brown rice, kept hot
2	green onions, sliced on the diagonal into 1/2 inch pieces
1 cup	golden currants
1 Tbsp	coconut oil
1/4 cup	slivered almonds or raw cashews

Sauce

1 cup	water
3 Tbsp	frozen apple or pineapple juice concentrate
2 Tbsp	tamari sauce
2 Tbsp	arrowroot
1/4 tsp	ground ginger
1/4 tsp	ground cinnamon
1/8 tsp	cayenne powder

Directions

· Cut chicken breast into 1 inch pieces and set aside.

· In a small bowl, mix together the ingredients for the sauce: cold water, juice concentrate, tamari sauce, arrowroot, ginger, cinnamon, and cayenne pepper.

· Preheat a large skillet or wok over medium-high heat. Add almonds or cashews and cook for a few minutes until golden. Remove skillet from the heat and take out the nuts.

· Pour coconut oil into the skillet. Add mushrooms and stir-fry until they release their water and are slightly browned.

· Pour in more cooking oil as needed.

· Add peppers and apples and stir-fry for 2 minutes until they are tender-crisp. Remove apple mixture and set aside with mushrooms.

· Add chicken pieces and stir-fry for 3 - 4 minutes until meat is no longer pink. Push chicken to the side of the skillet.

· Stir the sauce and add it to the middle of the skillet, cooking and stirring until it bubbles and becomes thick. Return the apple mixture to the skillet and then combine all the ingredients, coating everything with the sauce. Cook and stir until heated through.

· Toss in the nuts and serve over the hot cooked basmati brown rice.

· **NOTE:** One pound of white fish such as halibut may be used instead of chicken. Cut in 1 inch pieces and follow the same instructions as for above. Any other meat may also be used this stir-fry recipe.

ratatouille - a vegetable stew

Ingredients

1	large green pepper
1	large red pepper
2	medium zucchini
2	celery stalks
2	small eggplants
2	large yellow onions
2 1/2 lbs	ripe tomatoes
2-3	cloves garlic, crushed
1/2 tsp	oregano
1/2 tsp	thyme
1/2 tsp	dried basil (2 tsp minced fresh basil)
1/2 tsp	sea salt
1/2 tsp	fresh ground black pepper
1/4 cup	olive oil

Garnish

2 Tbsp	finely chopped parsley

Ratatouille is a versatile dish which can be used as a main course, and any left-overs can be re-heated as a topping for chicken, beef, and fish dishes, or served as a cold dip for vegetables and crackers.

Directions

· Prepare the eggplants first. Cut them into 3/4-inch cubes, place them in a colander, sprinkle with salt, and let drain for half an hour.

· Cut the peppers lengthwise into 2 inch strips. Slice the onions thickly. Dice the celery and crush the garlic. Coarsely chop the tomatoes. Slice the zucchini in half lengthwise and cut crosswise into 1/2 inch slices.

· Heat 1 Tbsp of the olive oil in a large, heavy skillet.

· Sauté the onions, celery, and peppers until the onions are translucent. Add the garlic and tomatoes. Cook and stir for about 3 - 5 minutes. Put the cooked mixture in a separate bowl.

· Add another Tbsp of oil to the skillet and sauté the zucchini for at least 10 minutes, and add to the cooked vegetables in the bowl.

· Using paper towels, drain and dry the diced eggplant.

· Add the rest of the olive oil to the skillet and sauté the eggplant for about 10 minutes.

· Return all the vegetables to the skillet and mix well. Cook the entire mixture for 5 minutes, stirring in the seasonings.

· Serve hot or very well chilled.

shepherdess pie - comfort food

Ingredients

(Serves 4-6)

Filling:

1 cup	green or brown lentils
1 Tbsp	extra virgin olive oil
1	large onion, peeled and chopped
5	garlic cloves, peeled and minced
3	carrots, diced
2	celery stalks, diced
10	mushrooms, quartered
1	red or green bell pepper, diced
1 cup	peas
1	tomato
1/2 tsp	dried or fresh basil
1/2 tsp	dried or fresh oregano
	sea salt and cracked pepper to taste
1/2 cup	fresh parsley, minced
1 Tbsp	tamari (optional)
1/4 tsp	cayenne pepper
	pinch of nutmeg
	juice of one lemon

Topping:

3	large potatoes, red or white
2	yams
1 Tbsp	extra virgin olive oil
1/2 cup	rice, nut milk, or the water that the potatoes cooked in sea salt and cracked pepper to taste. Optional: paprika.

Directions

· Rinse the lentils in water a couple of times and then boil them in water until they are just tender. Drain, rinse, and set aside.

· In a large frying pan fry the onions and garlic in the olive oil for about 3 minutes or until onions are translucent. Add carrots, celery, mushrooms, and bell pepper and sauté for 5-7 minutes. Then add all remaining ingredients for the filling and continue cooking for a few minutes.

· In the meantime, cut potatoes and yams into 1-inch cubes, leaving the skins on, and boil in water until soft. Drain and mash potatoes and yams with the oil, milk or water, salt and pepper until creamy and fluffy.

· Put the filling into a glass baking dish and top with mashed potatoes. Sprinkle with paprika and bake in preheated oven at 350° F for 20 minutes. Serve and enjoy!

Contributed by Commonsense Cookery, Victoria, BC

sweet smoky oven-baked beans

Ingredients

(Serves 8-10)

4 cups	black beans, soaked in water overnight
1 Tbsp	cumin powder
2 Tbsp	chili powder
6-8	garlic cloves, peeled and minced
1	large onion (red or yellow)
1 Tbsp	sea salt
2 Tbsp	chipotle purée (1 x 7oz. can chipotle chilies in adobo sauce (blend or chop finely)
1/3 cup	pure maple syrup
15 1/2 oz	can tomato paste
1/4 cup	apple cider vinegar
1 Tbsp	unsulfured molasses
	juice of 1 lime

Directions

· Preheat the oven to 350° F

· Place the soaked beans in a large pot and cover with cold water by one inch.

· Bring to a boil, reduce heat and simmer until beans are tender (about one hour or longer).

· Add more water to keep beans covered if necessary.

· Add 2 tsp sea salt in the final 15 minutes of cooking.

· Stir the remaining ingredients into the pot of beans. Put the beans into a glass baking dish, cover and bake for 1-2 hours until beans are at the desired consistency (not runny). Let sit for about 10 minutes before serving.

Contributed by Commonsense Cookery, Victoria, BC

lentil tomato - vegetable soup / stew

Ingredients

(Makes 8 to 10 servings)

8 cups	water or vegetable stock
2 cups	dry brown lentils
28 oz can	organic crushed tomatoes
1	large onion, chopped
4	cloves garlic, minced
2	celery stalks, chopped
4	carrots, chopped
1 Tbsp	olive oil
1-3 Tbsp	tamari sauce (organic and wheat-free)
1 tsp	sea salt, basil, and oregano
1/2 tsp	marjoram or thyme
2 Tbsp	parsley, chopped
	Cayenne pepper or tabasco to taste

Directions

· Wash and pick over the lentils. Cover them with 8 cups of water in a large pot. Cook for 30 minutes over medium heat.

· While cooking, sauté onion, garlic, celery, and carrots in olive oil.

· Add the sautéed vegetables, and the tomatoes to the lentils and cook for another 30 minutes or more, until the lentils are tender.

· Add the herbs and tamari sauce and continue cooking on low heat for about 25-30 minutes, until the vegetables are tender. Stir occasionally.

· Serve with flat bread.

From Laurell's kitchen

sweet potato tangy carrot crisp

Ingredients

(Makes 8 to 10 servings)

5	large sweet potatoes (about 2.5 lb)
12	carrots (about 2 lb)
3/4 cup	pineapple juice
2 Tbsp	unpasteurized liquid honey
2 Tbsp	safflower oil
2 tsp	cinnamon
2	cloves of garlic, minced
1 tsp	sea salt

Topping

1 1/2 cups	fresh rice bread crumbs or crushed rice cracker crumbs
1/2 cup	chopped pecans
1/3 cup	melted clarified butter or safflower oil
1 Tbsp	chopped fresh parsley

Directions

· Peel and cut sweet potatoes and carrots into large chunks. In large pot of boiling water, cook potatoes and carrots for about 20 minutes or until very tender; drain. Purée in food processor or blender, in batches if necessary.

· Add juice, honey, butter or oil, cinnamon, garlic and salt; blend well. Spoon into greased 13 x 9 inch baking dish

· Topping: Combine bread crumbs, pecans, oil and parsley and cover the potato-carrot mixture. Cover with foil and bake in 350° oven for 20 minutes. Uncover and bake for half an hour, or until heated through.

desserts
& treats

"No one needs desserts. They do not appear on any nutritionist's list of essential foods. But no one can deny the deep sweet satisfaction of a dessert. A good dessert make us feel good, like a good hug."

The following selection of desserts and treats provides healthy (and sweet!) options for the sweet-tooth types in your family, many of which can be eaten in moderation during the Elimination Test Diet. There are dessert recipes for special occasions, as well as every day bars and treats which can be easily slipped into school lunches. Remember that fruits and nuts are ready-to-go treats that require little or no extra preparation.

sunflower, pecan, apple & apricot crumble

Ingredients

Filling

1/4 cup	dried unsulfited apricots
1 lb	fresh fruit, such as: apples, cherries, and apricots, pitted and roughly chopped (Variations: black currants or cranberries, mixed with 1/2 cup dried apricots)

Topping

1/3 cup	oat flour
1 1/2 Tbsp	sunflower oil
1/4 cup	sunflower seeds, coarsely ground
1/4 cup	rolled oats
1/4 cup	pecans, finely ground
1 tsp	Stevia

Directions

· Preheat oven to 375° F

· Place the dried apricots in saucepan, cover with water, bring to a boil, and simmer for 5 minutes. Drain and add fresh cold water to cover the apricots.

· Return to a boil, reduced the heat, and simmer, covered, for 20 minutes or until tender.

· Add the remaining fruit to the apricots and cook, covered, for 5 minutes.

· Drain the fruit, reserving the liquid. Cut each of the dried apricots into 3 or 4 pieces. Place the fruit in a baking dish with 2/3 cup of the cooking liquid.

· For the topping, put the flour in a bowl and pour in the oil. Stir in the sunflower seeds, oats, ground pecans and the Stevia.

· Spread topping over the fruit. Bake for 15 minutes, or until golden. Serve hot.

 **fruit pick-ups**

Ingredients

(Makes 8 to 9 servings)

1	whole fresh pineapple, or honeydew melon
1 cup	honey
1 cup	sesame seeds and/or unsulfited short, shredded desiccated coconut

Directions

For pineapple:

· Pare and core the pineapple. Cut it into pieces about 2 inches square. Insert a toothpick into each square. Warm the honey in a saucepan. (Do not boil).

· Dip the pineapple squares into the honey and roll them in seeds. If desired, put them in the freezer to harden.

For melon:

· Use a melon baller to make little balls which can be dipped in the warm honey and rolled in seeds or the coconut.

cashew halvah

Ingredients

(Makes 36 squares)

1 cup	sesame seeds
1 cup	chopped raisins (packed)
2/3 cup	water
1/2 tsp	vanilla extract
1/8 tsp	almond extract
1/3 cup	tahini
1 cup	unsalted cashews, finely chopped or ground

Directions

- Prepare an 8 x 8 inch square pan with oil or lecithin oil. Set aside.

- In a large saucepan, combine sesame seeds, raisins and water. Bring mixture to a boil over high heat, and cook for 2 or 3 minutes. Then stir in extracts and tahini.

- Continue cooking and stirring for another 1 or 2 minutes. Stir in cashews.

- Remove from heat. Pat firmly and evenly into prepared pan.

- Refrigerate at least 1 hour before cutting. Cut into small squares and store in airtight container or individually wrapped.

sweet potato chips

Ingredients

1 1/4 lb   orange-fleshed sweet
potatoes

1-2 Tbsp   safflower oil

Optional: Cinnamon

Directions

·   Peel the sweet potatoes. Cut them into
lengthwise strips. Then cut into fat 1/2 inch
square chips.

·   In a large, heavy-bottomed skillet, heat the
oil and stir-fry the potatoes over high heat
for 8 - 9 minutes, until just tender and
blistered in places.

·   Sprinkle cinnamon on chips if desired.

sesame bars - lots!

Ingredients:

DRY

9 cups	sesame seeds
3 cups	sunflower seeds
2 cups	coconut
2 cups	barley flour
1 cup	roasted peanuts or cashews
1/2 tsp	sea salt
	(pine nuts, slivered almonds, crushed hazelnuts, or pumpkin seeds may be substituted or added for a 'gourmet' bar)

WET

1 cup	barley malt
1 1/2	cups almond butter, or cashew butter* (or replace 1/2 cup with mashed banana)
2 3/4	Honey or maple syrup
1 1/2 Tbsp	pure vanilla extract
	safflower oil

Directions

- PREHEAT oven to 400°

- Oil two large cookie sheets with the safflower oil.

- Mix all DRY ingredients in a large bowl. Stir well.

- Mix all WET ingredients in a large saucepan on the stove over medium low heat. Stir until well combined.

- Add DRY ingredients from the large bowl into the WET ingredients on the stove.

- Stir until the mixture is thoroughly mixed and produces a sticky consistency. Add more DRY or WET ingredients as needed.

- Use a large spoon or ladle to transfer the mixture to the cookie sheets

- Press the mixture into the cookie sheets with a rolling pin to make a smooth, flat surface

- BAKE at 325° for 10 - 15 minutes

- Allow the bars to cool in the pans. Use a pizza cutter to cut the baked mixture into 48 pieces (6 x 8) or 96 pieces (3 x 4) and remove the bars from the trays with a metal spatula.

- CUT into 48 pieces (6 x 8) or 96 (3 x 4)

*Peanut butter may replace almond or cashew butter after the Elimination Test Diet is completed, and there is no allergic response.

earth balls

Ingredients

(Makes between 15 - 30 balls)

Try to use unsulfured dried fruit for this recipe

(5 oz) 3/4 cups currants

(5 oz) 3/4 cups dried figs

(4 oz) 1/2 cups cooking dates

(1 1/2 oz)
1/8-1/4 cups   walnuts, chopped

(1 1/2 oz)
1/8-1/4 cups   sunflower seeds

Ground cinnamon and/or desiccated coconut for dusting.

Directions

·   In a food processor or blender, first process the nuts until they are finely ground.

·   Add in the dried fruit gradually, and process until the mixture is well combined. Add more nuts if the mixture is too sticky.

·   Shape into 2 inch diameter balls and roll them in cinnamon or coconut, depending on your preference.

·   These Earth Balls make delicious traveling snacks and store well in the refrigerator until they are discovered!

*The ounces (oz) in this recipe refer to the ounces marked on the food processor feeder tube, as this is how the recipe was originally created.

brown rice crispies

Ingredients

(Makes 24 squares)

1 tsp	unrefined sesame oil
1/2 cup	brown rice syrup or honey
1 Tbsp	almond butter or sesame tahini
1 tsp	pure vanilla extract
3 cups	dry natural brown rice crispy cereal*

Optional additions:

1/2 cup	raisins or currants
1/4 cup	almonds, sesame seeds or sunflower seeds

Directions

· Put oil in a large pot and heat.

· Add rice syrup and nut butter.

· Stir and heat until bubbles form.

· Turn off heat and add vanilla.

· Add cereal and mix well with a spatula.

· Stir in optional items and mix lightly.

· Press into a 8 x 8 in pan. Use slightly wet hands to press mixture flat. Let mixture set to room temperature.

· Cut into slices or squares and serve.

* Purchase at health food store or health food section at the supermarket.

244

gingery fresh fruit salad

Ingredients

(Makes 6 Servings)

Always try to use fruits and berries which are in season.

1	pear, peeled, cored and cut into 1/2″ pieces
1	green apple, quartered, cored and cut into 1/2″ pieces
2	ripe peaches, pitted and cut into 1/2″ pieces
2	cups blue berries or 1 1/2 cups strawberries, sliced, chopped
3 Tbsp	fresh lemon juice
4 cups	water
2 Tbsp	julienned lemon zest*
3 inch	length of fresh ginger root, finely grated
2/3 cup	Sucanat

* Orange zest can be substituted when the Elimination Test Diet is completed.

Directions

- Place all the cut fruit and berries in a large bowl. Pour the lemon juice over the fruit and toss well. Place the bowl in the mid range of the refrigerator.

- Pour 4 cups of water into a large saucepan over medium-high heat. Add the lemon zest, grated ginger, and sucanat.

- Bring the mixture to a boil. Reduce the heat and simmer the liquid until it is reduced to 2 cups of syrup. Remove the ginger.

- Pour the syrup into a large bowl and let stand at room temperature until it cools. Add the chilled fruit to the syrup and stir to coat the fruit. Put the bowl of fruit back in the refrigerator, cover it and chill the fruit for about an hour and a half.

toasted nuts and seeds

Directions

Toasted nuts and seeds can be tossed on most salads for extra flavour, nutrition, and crunch. They also make handy snacks in lunch boxes and when hiking.

Any preferred combination of walnuts, cashews, brazil nuts, hazel nuts, almonds, pecans, (and peanuts)*, pumpkin seeds and sunflower seeds may be toasted in a dry frying pan over medium heat.

Stir the combination often until lightly browned for 3 - 5 minutes. Remove from the heat and stir in tamari sauce to taste, adding any of your favourite spices.

* If tolerated.

refreshing
beverages

"Tea tempers the spirit, harmonizes the mind, dispels lassitude and relieves fatigue, awakens the thoughts and prevents drowsiness."

Lu Yu, The Chinese Art of Tea

Food IQ Information

Most commercial fruit juices are heavily laden with pesticides and are made mostly with unfiltered water and added sugars. Pop is akin to "liquid candy" with most soft drinks containing at least 1.2 teaspoons of sugar per ounce. At most fast-food restaurants, the child's soft-drink portion is usually twelve ounces, the small size, sixteen ounces, and the large serving is thirty-two fluid ounces. North Americans drink twice as much pop as milk and about six times more pop than juice. For teen-age boys and girls, about 40% of their daily sugar consumption comes from soft drinks.

morrocan mint tea

Ingredients

(Serves 4 to 6)

2 tsp	green tea
1/4 cup	spearmint leaves, dried or 8 leaves of fresh spearmint
1/4 cup	unpasteurized honey
	boiling water

Directions

· Preheat a teapot with boiling water.

· Pour out the water and place the green tea in the warmed pot.

· Pour 1/2 cup of boiling water over the tea. Allow to sit 2 minutes.

· Pour off the water, leaving the tea leaves in the pot.

· Place the spearmint in the pot, and pour boiling water over the mint and green tea. Stir the tea well, and allow it to steep for 3 - 5 minutes. Remove any mint floating on the top of the tea.

· Add the honey and mix it in well.

· Serve hot in small cups or glasses.

herbal iced teas

Ingredients

Herbal berry and fruit flavoured teas make delicious iced teas.

Rose-hip, apple, lemon, orange, blueberry, raspberry, blackcurrant, and blackberry are some of the many choices now widely available.

Directions

· To make a pitcher of tea, use a ratio of one cup of brewed tea to eight cups of water, plus ice.

· In a saucepan, add one tea bag of choice and one cup of water. Bring to a simmer over medium-high heat and simmer for at least 10 minutes. Allow tea to cool. In a glass pitcher, add 8 cups of chilled water and some ice.

· The tea can be sweetened by adding honey to taste while it is still warm, or you may add drops of Stevia liquid extract to taste.

· **NOTE:** Too much Stevia can make the tea taste bitter.

· Serve in tall glasses with fresh fruit, berry, and mint garnishes whenever possible.

chamomile comforter

Ingredients

(Makes 4 servings)

2 1/2 cups water

1 1/2 cups organic apple juice

2 tea bags chamomile tea

1   1 inch slice fresh
            ginger

            orange slices for
            garnish

Directions

· Combine the water and the apple juice in a small saucepan and bring to a simmer. Add the tea bags and ginger, cover with a lid, and continue to simmer for 8 - 10 minutes.

· Strain the tea into a preheated teapot and serve with orange slices.

· A winter version of this tea may include adding a cinnamon stick and a clove during the simmering process.

OR

· You may refrigerate this tea and add ice cubes, for a hot summer day cooler for both adults and children. This tea served warm is especially great for children when they need calming, have tummy aches, or when they just need comfort. Peter Rabbit's mother knew this very well!

sparkling strawberry lemonade

Ingredients

(Makes 4 servings)

3/4 cup	honey
1/2 cup	water
2 cups	rinsed, stemmed and chopped strawberries
1 cup	strained fresh lemon juice
24 oz	sparkling water
	mint leaves

Directions

· Combine the honey and water in a small saucepan on medium heat.

· Stir continuously until blended.

· Transfer syrup to a blender, add the strawberries and lemon juice and purée until well blended.

· Combine the purée with the sparkling water and serve in tall glasses over ice. Garnish with mint leaves.

TIP: To get the maximum juice from your lemons, bathe them in warm water for 10 minutes before squeezing them.

· Variations: Two cups of raspberries or blackberries, or one cup of blueberries can be substituted for strawberries.

"When life gives you lemons, make lemonade!"
Erma Bombeck

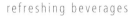

ginger ale

Ingredients

4 cups	water
3/4 cup	ginger root, peeled and chopped
2 Tbsp	pure vanilla extract
1 Tbsp	pure lemon extract
1/2 tsp	stevia powder
	Carbonated, sparkling water

Directions

· This is both refreshing and great for upset tummies.

almond berry smoothie

Ingredients

(Makes one 12 oz serving)

1/2 cup	frozen berries (your choice)
1/2	banana, frozen
10	pre-soaked almonds* (whole and raw)
1/2 cup	rice or nut milk
1/2	organic apple juice

Making this smoothie requires soaking almonds two days in advance.

Directions

How to soak almonds:

· Place almonds (whole raw) in a small container and cover with fresh cold water.

· Soak in refrigerator for two days. Top up with water when necessary.

At the same time:

· Peel the banana, put it inside a ziplock bag and place it in the freezer. If using fresh berries, make sure you freeze them as well.

For the Smoothie:

· When ready to make your smoothie, place all the above ingredients in a blender.

· Mix on high until almonds are puréed to a smooth consistency.

*Soaked almonds should last about a week if kept cold and rinsed well.

from Carol Mann's 'Earthshake Café', Parksville, B.C.

WEEKLY MENU PLAN

Meals	Monday	Tuesday	Wednesday
Breakfast			
Mid-Morning Snack			
Lunch			
After-School Snack			
Supper			

Thursday	Friday	Saturday	Sunday

NOTES

NOTES

NOTES

References

· Boris, M. (1994) Foods and food additives are common causes of attention deficit hyperactivity disorder in children. *Annals of Allergy, 72,* 462-68.

· Crawford, M. (1993) The role of essential fatty acids in neural development: Implications for perinatal nutrition. *American Journal of Clinical Nutrition*, 5, 703S-709S.

· Galland, L. (1988) *Superimmunity for Kids: What to Feed Your Children to Keep Them Healthy Now – and Prevent Disease in Their Future.* New York: Delta Publishing.

· Gioanni, M. (1997) *The Complete Food Allergy Cookbook.* Prima Health Publishing.

· Gleason, P. & Suitor, C. (2001) *Food for Thought: Children's Diets in the 1990s.* Princeton: Mathematica Policy Research, Inc. (www.mathematica-mpr.com)

· Heimburger, D.C., Satllings, V.A.& Routzahn, L. (1998). Survey of clinical nutrition training programs for physicians. *American Journal of Clinical Nutrition*, 68, 1174-9.

· Joneja, J. (1997) *Dietary Management of Food Allergies and Intolerances.* British Columbia: J.A.Hall Publications, Ltd.

· Richardson, A.J., Puri, BK. (2002) A randomized double-blind, placebo-controlled study of the effects of supplementation with highly unsaturated fatty acids on adhd-related symptoms in children with specific learning disabilities. *Prog Neuropsychopharmacol Biol Psychiatry* 2002; 26 (2): 233-239

· Robbins, J. (1992) *May All be Fed: Diet for a New World.* New York: Avon Books.

· Sears, B. (2002) the *Omega Rx Zone*. New York: Regan Books.

· Simontacchi, C. (2000) *The Crazy Makers: How the Food Industry is Destroying Our Brains and Harming Our Children.* New York: Penguin Putnam.

· Stevens, L.J., et al. (1995) Essential Fatty Acid Metabolism in Boys with Attention Deficit Hyperactivity Disorder. American *Journal of Clinical Nutrition.* 1995. 62 (4): 761-68

· Stordy, J.B. (1997) Essential Fatty Acids (EFA's) and learning disorders. Holistic *Health Journal*, Oct. 1997

· Vallejo F, Tomas-Barberan FA, Garcia-Viguera C, et al. (2003) Phenolic compound contents in edible parts of broccoli inflorescences after domestic cooking. *Journal of the Science and Food Agricultural Volume,* 14:1511-1516

· Zimmerman, M. (1999) *The A.D.D. Nutrition Solution: A Drug-Free 30-Day Nutrition Solution.* New York: Henry Holt & Company.

Recommended Resources

· Barstsow, C. (2002) *The Eco-Foods Guide: What's good for the Earth is Good for You.* Gabriola Island: New Society.

· Bateson-Koch, C. (1994) *Allergies: Disease in Disguise.* Burnaby: Alive Books.

· Brostoff, J. & Gamlin, L. (2000) *The Complete Guide to Food Allergy and Intolerance: Prevention, Identification, and Treatment of Common Illnesses and Allergies caused by Food. New York:* Inner Traditions Intl., Ltd.

· Dumke, N. M. (1992) *Allergy Cooking with Ease.* PA: Starburst Publishing.

· Dumke, N. M. (1997) *Easy Breadmaking for Special Diets.* Allergy Adapt, Inc.

· Dumke, N. M. (1998) *5 Years Without Food - The Food Allergy Survival Guide: How to Overcome Your Food Allergies and Recover Good Health.* Allergy Adapt, Inc.

· Galland, L. (1988) *Superimmunity for Kids: What to Feed Your Children to Keep Them Healthy Now –* and Prevent Disease in Their Future. New York: Delta Publishing.

· Gioanni, M. (1997) *The Complete Food Allergy Cookbook.* Prima Health Publishing.

· Hurt-Jones, M. (2001) *The Allergy Self-Help Cookbook:* Over 325 Natural Food Recipes, Free of all Common Food Allergens. Rodale Press.

· Krohn, J. (1996) *The Whole Way to Allergy Relief and Prevention.* Vancouver: Hartley and Marks Publishers.

· Lewis, L. (1998) *Special Diets for Special Kids: Understanding and Implementing Special Diets to Aid in the Treatment of Autism and Related Developmental Disorders.* Arlington: Future Horizons.

· Lyon, M.R. (2000) *Healing the Hyperactive Brain.* Calgary. Focused Publishing.

· Martin, Jeanne Marie (1997) *The All Natural Allergy Cookbook.* Harbour Pub, Co.

· Page Johnson, D. (2001) *The Feel Good Food Guide: Easy Recipes Free of Sugar, Wheat, Yeast, Corn, Eggs, Dairy and Soy!* Michigan: Sheridan Books. (www.feelgoodfood.com)

· Rapp, D.J. (1996) *Is This Your Child's World?* New York: Bantam Books.

· Robbins, J. (1992) *May All be Fed: Diet for a New World.* New York: Avon Books.

· Schwartz, R. (2003) *The Enlightened Eater's Whole Foods Guide: Harvest the Power of Phyto Foods.* Viking Books.

- Simontacchi, C. (2000) *The Crazy Makers: How the Food Industry is Destroying Our Brains and Harming Our Children.* New York: Penguin Putnam.

- Warrington, J. (1991) *Sweet & Natural: Desserts without Sugar, Honey, Molasses, or Artificial Sweeteners.* California: The Crossing Press.

- Zimmerman, M. (1999) *The A.D.D. Nutrition Solution: A Drug-Free 30-Day Nutrition Solution.* New York: Henry Holt & Company.

Related Magazines and Websites

Additive Alert: What Have They Done to Our Food? (1994) Pollution Probe, McClelland & Stewart, Inc.

The Complete Food Guide: The Shopper's Guide to More than 1,000 Ingredients. (1999) QA International, Quebec. (www.qa-international.com)

Eating Well: The Magazine of Food and Health (www.eatingwell.com)

Food Allergy Network (www.foodallergy.org)

Canadian Celiac Association (www.celiac.ca)

Gluten Free Group of North America (www.gluten.net)

Living Without: A Lifestyle Guide for People with Food and Chemical Sensitivities (published quarterly, contains allergy free recipes: (www.livingwithout.com)

RECIPE INDEX